T0157547

A Time to Remember

The Life and Times of La Vellea Samot

La Vellea Samot

authorHOUSE®

AuthorHouse™
1663 Liberty Drive
Bloomington, IN 47403
www.authorhouse.com
Phone: 1 (800) 839-8640

Published by AuthorHouse 10/05/2015

ISBN: 978-1-5049-1623-3 (sc)
ISBN: 978-1-5049-1622-6 (e)

Print information available on the last page.

This book is printed on acid-free paper.

Contents

This book is dedicated to my mother and my grandmother who taught me that education would unlock doors for me. I loved them and still do love them even though they have gone to be with the Lord. They were women of wisdom and integrity. With the help of God, they always guided me in the direction that they knew would get me to where I wanted to go without being in harms way.

PREFACE

"A Time To Remember: The Life and Times of La Vellea Samot" is a captivating biography of a young woman born in the deep roots of the south and how she used life's lemons, hardships, and bad times to flourish and make something out of a life destined to never change.

Chapter 1

NATURE INSPIRED REFLECTION

The sun was just hitting the crest of the horizon as I was awakened from my slumber by God's hand. It was shining through the cedar bushes outside my patio doors causing them to cast their shadow through the curtains. The wind blew softly through the bushes causing them to sway from side to side as if they were doing a ceremonial dance celebrating the rising of the sun and the beginning of a new day.

I laid there as I gazed at the beauty of nature and all of its inhabitants. As I looked out the window at the bushes I found myself marveling at their beautiful precision and graceful movements as the wind blew softly through them. The tree limbs moved up and down waving their leaves as though they were rejoicing and giving praise just for the opportunity to be a living object. Two little furry squirrels with beautiful bushy tails caught my attention as they chased each other on the rails of my patio. I watched these agile creatures as the sun cast their shadows against my curtains. They were running as if they were competing in a marathon. Although I wanted to see which one won the race I could not help but look up at the sky as the sun was now totally exposed from its slumber as well. I have to admit that it was possibly the most beautiful blue sky I had ever seen. There was not a cloud in the sky. The grass wet with dew, glistened as if each blade had been covered in diamonds. The birds were joyfully singing and happily flying from one tree to another. I did not know the origin of all the aeronautical creatures that were performing a symphony of nature's music with their unique chirping and audible sounds. They seemed to be utilizing every ounce of energy they possessed to perform a duty that seemed to announce to the world that a new day is beginning, yesterday is gone, and tomorrow is not promised. It seemed as if this day had been given to me to reflect on the past and plan for my future. The beautiful dance nature displayed for the world to see inspired me to move quickly to ready myself for the day because I did not want to waste a minute of it. I knew that when this day was gone it would be gone forever.

"What a beautiful day to be alive!" I said out loud. Thinking, I must get myself together, get showered, dressed, and begin my day. It was imperative that I plan what I was going to do today and begin working toward the goals I had set. I knew I had to plan to work efficiently and with purpose to insure there would not be a minute to regret at the end of the day. As I prepared, my mind began to drift for some reason. The nostalgic feeling of this day was familiar. I was reminded of the similar feeling I had some forty years ago. That feeling came from a time my mother had spent a full summer with my husband and me.

This summer was very interesting because my mother allowed us to be her audience as she shared numerous stories as we sat attentively listening to her every word. Her reflection and candidness gave us a glimpse into her life that spanned from the Great Depression to the Civil Rights Movement. Not to mention that her family history dealt with everything from the story of the pain brought to the family by a family member, her marriage to our dad, our birth, her divorce, and a myriad of other mother-only secrets that she had never revealed to me before. Every day as she was a narrator of this particular time in history, she would tell me more about her life and the things that happened in her siblings' lives as well.

I looked forward to having our talks in the evenings and I learned many things about my mother and her life that I did not know. I relished in the fact that I was able to receive such intimate details from her in this summer of what I called an awakening to a time and place where I once lived. I was unaware of so many facets of the woman who guided and raised me.

As I looked at the clock and prepared my day, I was reminded that this day had been so familiar even though mom had been deceased for 20 years. Snapping my mind back to reality from this nature inspired reflective moment; I had to realize that this was the beginning of a trip down memory lane that would open up the doors to my soul and my past.

Chapter 2

THE DAY WITH PAPA

It was a Saturday morning and I had made a mental note of all the things I had planned to do for the day. First, I need to go to the grocery store. I had worked all week and I was too tired to go to the grocery store on Friday evening. We were out of milk, bread, and eggs. I was truly surprised as I checked our coffee supply and found that we were completely out. This was not going to work! I can do without eggs. I can even do without milk. But being without coffee was an abomination! My husband and I needed our coffee to get our adrenaline going. In our house, it was a cardinal sin to run out of coffee.

I knew immediately that I needed to hurry, shower, get dressed, check the refrigerator and cabinets to see what else we needed, make a list of these things, and get myself to the grocery store expeditiously. Although the urgency to run off to the grocery store was present; I seemingly could not move from the spot where I had the first revelation of my mother. Perhaps the spot where I stood every morning would become the spot where I would meet with Mother's voice and the memories of my past. As I stood there and allowed myself time to remember what I had been told by my mother, the urgency for the daily requirements from the grocery store and the thought of coffee were no match for the powerful beckoning of my past at this necessary moment of reflection. Before I knew it, the thought of coffee evaporated from my consciousness and my mother's voice took center stage of my thoughts.

Some of the things my mother told me happened before I was born and some after, but I was not old enough to know what was happening. For instance on this day, I thought about the things my mother told me about my grandfather, known to me as Papa.

Mother's father was the youngest of sixteen children. He was born to parents who were former slaves. Papa's father had four brothers and since no one knew who their father was, it was assumed that they were fathered by the slave master who owned a slave plantation. Papa's father died when he was eleven years old and he was raised by his three older brothers, all of whom were former slaves. My grandfather, excuse me, my Papa spent most of his young adult years in Kosko. Prior to meeting and marrying my grandmother, Papa was married to another wonderful woman and they had a son. When the baby was six months old, he and his mother went to visit family members who lived a short distant from their home. On their way back, he and his mother got caught in a heavy rain storm. She came down with pneumonia and died several weeks later. This left a small baby boy without a mother. So, Papa took the responsibility to raise Uncle Troy along with the help of his mother and other family members.

A year later, in 1909, Papa met my grandmother. They were married on February 23, 1910, which transformed my grandmother to the more affectation name of Mama. Immediately Mama became the maternal influence for young Troy. She also began taking care of Papa's mother until her death in 1912. The bond between my grandmother and Uncle Troy was so evident that if you wanted to ruffle her feathers, all you had to do was refer to Uncle Troy as her stepson. As a matter of fact, I have many memories of my grandmother; but one that sticks out in particular is this one Sunday when most of the women came to her house. Her house was directly across the street from the church. On Sundays, they would grab a glass of cool water, along with refreshments and talk until it was time to go back to church. Up until this Sunday,

I had never seen my sweet, loving Grandmother ever get mad. That is until I heard one of the women refer to Uncle Troy as Grandmother's stepson. My Grandmother's face turned beet red in the middle of this hot summer day, and she changed her loving face to a menacing scowl. She then looked at that woman and said, "There is no such thing as a stepson, he is my son!" Needless to say Grandmother truly loved Uncle Troy. She never referred to him as her stepson; he was her son. He was befitting of the title because at the time he did not know any mother but her. I'd like to think that it was not because Grandmother and Papa did not want him to know but because he was too young to understand and things just flowed naturally. This did not change even when eleven months later Grandmother gave birth to my mother, on January 15, 1911. The bond that my Grandmother shared with Uncle Troy was so strong that although my mother was maternally the first child born between Papa and Grandmother, they still considered her as their second child.

Grandmother and Papa were farmers by nature. They farmed the land owned by Papa's father, along with three of his brothers and several of his sisters and their husbands. Unfortunately, a few years after Mother was born, Papa's brothers got into a feud of some sorts. The feud was a mystery to most of the family; but it was such a mess that several of Papa's sisters and their families wanted to sell their part of the land. This placed Papa right in the middle of the feuding sisters and their families. So Papa gave them his part of the land and moved away because he did not want to be a part of a family feud. Papa moved his family to a small town in the Delta. Papa's sister and her husband also lived in the Delta. One of Papa's brothers moved to Birmingham, Alabama. No one maintained contact with him and he was never heard from again. His oldest brother and his wife moved to Arkansas. My mother never heard what happened to the third brother but it is suspected that he stayed in Kosko and died there. Papa kept in contact with his oldest brother up until about 1937; however, he lost contact with him after that year. Papa knew his oldest brother had a very large family so he tried to stay in contact with them throughout the years until his death in 1951.

CHAPTER 3

LIFE ON THE PLANTATION

Shortly after Papa and Grandmother moved to the Delta, they added three more additions to the family. They now had four children. Uncle Jessie was just an infant when Papa and Grandmother moved into the house with his sister and brother-in-law who lived on a local minister's plantation. Rev. Winston's Plantation was known as the Winston Plantation. Papa and Grandmother were proud parents. Yet, there was still a sadness and a heavy heart because they lost the child before Uncle Jessie whose name was **Earl**. This child was lost to a battle with diarrhea at the age of two. It was good that Papa and Grandmother were able to live with family until a house was built for them on the plantation. This helped them deal with the loss of a child while trying to maintain a normal family life.

Being a sharecropper on a plantation was not an easy life so my mother helped out in raising her younger two brothers, Uncle Myers and Uncle Jessie. Mother, now ten years old, found herself playing momma while her older brother, Uncle Troy, now twelve years old, was helping out Papa and Grandmother in the cotton fields.

Time on Mr. Winston's plantation was short lived. After just three short years, Papa and Grandmother moved a short distance from this plantation to another plantation owned by Mr. Bob Lockett, a black plantation owner. They lived and sharecropped on this farm for several years. There were a few blacks who owned farm land, but the white plantation owners outnumbered them. They did not refer to the blacks who owned land as plantation owners because of the size of their farms. They referred to them as "small farms". During the years from 1919 to 1927, four additional children were born to Grandmother and Papa. At this time, they lost two of their children. One was **Earl**, who died of diarrhea because the doctor could not stop it. The other was Ollie, who lived only a few hours and he died because the midwife cut his umbilical cord too short and he bled to death. Even in the middle of all this death, the fourth and last child born was a son, the youngest of all the children

During the fall of 1922, about three years after they started working on Mr. Lockett's Plantation, Papa and his family moved to another plantation known as the Brandon Place. It was three miles east of a small town known as **Huspuckena, Mississippi**. Mother said that there was an old tale (known as a wife's tale) told by many of the older people as to how this town got its name. Supposedly, the town did not have a name until one evening an Indian woman and her baby, along with other people, were fishing on the banks of a small creek in this no name portion of land. Her baby was lying in a straw basket and it kept crying. The baby's name was **Puckena**. After the baby had cried for quite some time she said, "**Hus Puckena**". People though that she was trying to say hush, but she kept saying, "**Hus Puckena**" over and over again. When the people fishing on the creek heard this, they decided to name the town **Huspuckena**. Mother said that she did not believe this tale to be true but all of her life she had heard it told by the older people over and over again.

Papa and his family lived on the Brandon Place for five years. They moved again during the fall of 1928 to the Baker Plantation which was not very far from the Lockett Plantation. They seemed to be moving around in circles, always moving close to the plantation they had left, but never returning to it. After moving to the Baker Plantation, Papa had worked very hard and had bought his own farm equipment and mules to farm the land he had rented to plant cotton and corn. Since Papa had used his own mules and equipment instead of the plantation owner's, he was to be compensated for using his own equipment. The plantation owner was supposed to deduct a portion of the rent that Papa owed him, thus Papa was to be given credit for the use of his own mules and plowing equipment; however, this did not happen. By using his own equipment, Papa's deductions would have gotten him out of most of his debt. At the end of the year he was not supposed to owe the owner much money. After Papa and his family began to gather the cotton and corn, the owner informed Papa that although he had gotten his rent and his money for the items that Papa had bought on credit, Papa would still owe him a significant amount of money. Papa told the owner that he was not going to finish gathering the crops and that he was going to move. The owner told Papa that if he moved and did not finish gathering the crops he would take his mules and plowing equipment. After giving much thought to the situation, the owner tried to make a deal with Papa knowing that he did not want to gather the crops that Papa would have left if he moved. The plantation owner asked Papa to stay in the house until the crops were gathered. If that was not an option, the owner asked if he and his family would come back and gather the crops although they had moved to another plantation. If Papa took the owner up on either one of these offers, the owner would not take Papa's mules and plowing equipment and would give him credit for the use of them. Seeing no positive way out of this situation, Papa decided to move to another plantation owned by Mr. D. J. Kerry, east of **Huspuckena**, but agreed to come back to the Baker Plantation every day and gather the crops until the debt was paid off at the end of the harvest.

Working in the cotton field was very hard work. Papa and his family had worked hard on every plantation they had lived on. There was no such thing as sleeping late in the mornings. Everyone was up at 4:00 a.m. The cows had to be milked, hogs fed, breakfast cooked and eaten, and they had to be in the field by 6:00 a.m. Papa had a total of six people to help him do the field work which included him, Grandmother, and their four children. When the family went to the field, the sun was not up but it was light enough for them to see how to do the work. They had to consume a good solid breakfast in order to help keep up the strength needed to complete the work they were required to do.

The list of post sunrise work that was required was long! The grass had to be hoed from around the small cotton plants. This came to about 30 acres. There were four children, all of whom were under 16 years old, to help with the work. The children were young, but they were hard workers. They knew that they needed to hoe as many rows of cotton as they possibly could for it to be considered a successful run of a day.

This was an arduous task every day. Though the mornings were cool, as the morning coolness faded, the hot sun would start shining on them as if God made it a spotlight directed right at them. So shade was a commodity in the open field. In order to make this laborious work somewhat manageable they wore wide brim straw hats to cover their heads from the sun and long sleeve shirts which helped to keep them cool when they started sweating. You might think that long sleeve shirts would make them even hotter, but that was not the case. The shirts with long sleeves held the sweat making the shirts damp with moisture. This gave the illusion of a damp rag that brushed the skin whenever wind would assist the movement of the fabric.

The hoeing of the cotton began the last week of March for another year. The tool used to remove the grass from around the cotton was known as a "hoe". The blade of a hoe was a long horizontal piece of metal with a round piece of metal attached to the back of the blade. The piece attached to the back of the blade was known as the neck of the hoe. A round wooden rod, called the "hoe handle" fit into the metal neck of the hoe. The blade of the hoe was sharpened with a metal file. The sharpened blade made it easier to cut the grass. One held on to the handle and pulled the blade between the cotton plants to remove the grass. Sometimes some of the cotton plants that were planted too thick had to be cut with the hoe in order to thin them out and give the plants ample room to grow.

When hoeing the cotton, Papa, Grandmother, and their older children could stand up straight pulling the hoe through the grass to cut it. When gathering the cotton, which the southerners referred to as "picking cotton", they had to bend over or they crawled on their knees when their backs became too tired from bending over. The younger children very seldom crawled on their knees because the cotton plants were the right height for them. The adults put on knee pads when they got on their knees to use as cushions. Knee pads were made of thick leather cut into squares with straps to fasten them on the knees. The pads either buckled or tied behind the knees to keep the pads in place. The sacks that the cotton was gathered in were nine feet in length and at least two feet wide. Think of filling a sack this size with cotton, putting one handful in at a time. The sacks were big and long, but could be filled to the very top. The cotton grew in to what was called a "boll". Many bolls of cotton were joined to the same stalk. When the bolls opened, there were five to six edges at each end. When Grandmother, Papa, and the children pulled the cotton from the bolls, the sharp, hard, pointed edges pierced the end of their fingers, and even went under their nails and cuticles causing them to bleed. At the end of each day, their fingers hurt so badly and were so sore that it was hard to keep going; nonetheless, they knew that they had to keep working because the cotton had to be gathered. To help heal the sore hands, Grandmother used beef fat to make what was called "tallow". Tallow was made by trimming the fat off of beef, frying it, draining the oil from it, and then adding turpentine. It was allowed to cool, was placed in a jar, and then used as a cream to apply to their sore fingers and cuticles each night before going to bed. Their fingers soon became tough and they were able to withstand the pain. Too much depended on the amount of cotton gathered. They could not afford to lose any of the cotton they had planted due to sore fingers. There was no time for crying or no option to call in for a sick day because the owners of the plantations had to collect money for the rent, any money borrowed, and for anything bought on credit. The amount of money left over for the sharecropper after he had taken care of his obligations was used to buy clothes and shoes for his family and food that could not be grown.

Even though my mother did not go to the field, she had to continue her babysitting duties. Her babysitting duties did not keep her from doing her work around the house. The beds had to be made, dishes washed and put away, bedroom floors swept, and the kitchen floor swept and mopped. When her baby sister and brother awoke, they needed to be cleaned, dressed, and fed. There was no idle time. Sitting around and not doing something productive with your hands was not an option.

Every day at 9:00 a.m., Grandmother left the field and went home to cook dinner. My mother could help cook, but she was not allowed to start dinner on her own even though she was old enough and knew how to cook. Grandmother felt that Mother could not successfully watch two small active children and cook at the same time. She felt that she might burn the house down and burn herself up along with her siblings. At 12:00 noon, Papa and the other children came home from the fields to eat dinner. Dinner was their heaviest meal next to breakfast. After dinner was eaten, they laid on the floor to rest until approximately 1:30 p.m. At this time, they returned to the field to work until it was too dark to even see how to work. After the light was dimmed by the sun setting, the work was not done! Only the field work was done for the day, but now the evening chores had to be done before going to bed. The hogs had to be fed and the cows had to be milked again. The second milking in the evening was important because the morning helping of milk garnered from the cows was not enough to fulfill the supply of milk needed for the family's milk and butter. In addition to those chores the chicken nests were checked once more for eggs that the hens may have laid after the morning gathering.

After gathering the evening eggs, the hen house doors had to be closed to keep the dogs, foxes, and weasels from getting inside to kill and eat the chickens during the night. This process was also necessary for the chicken coupes that housed the small baby chickens.

After tending to all the animals on the farm, wood had to be chopped to make a fire for the wood stove used to cook breakfast and dinner for the next day. In addition to replenishing the wood supply they also replenished the water supply. Water had to be pumped for evening and morning use. Although dinner was consumed at 12'o clock and done shortly after; cooking supper was hardly ever finished at one setting. If anyone was hungry after finishing the evening chores they would have to eat either cornbread with butter, syrup along with buttermilk, or a baked sweet potato with sugar and butter.

In addition to the home grown crops and supplies the family grew to sustain them, many sharecroppers lived on plantations where the owners had small grocery stores. Many took up food on credit and had to pay that bill and the rent for the use of the land out of their profit. Some found themselves with not enough money to carry them through the winter months and had to borrow against the next year's crop. The plantation owners kept a ledger to keep track of what each sharecropper owed. When the crops were gathered and the sharecroppers went to pay what was due, the plantation owner would pull out his ledger and say "Del". Even though the sharecropper's name was Delvin, the owner could shorten the name if he wanted. Many of the plantation owners would say something like, "You borrowed $200 to buy plowing equipment, cotton seed, corn seed, and fertilizer. You borrowed another $150 to buy clothes and shoes for your family. You charged $100 worth of food supplies for you and your family. Now, let's see, you owe me $450."

For some sharecroppers, after paying the rent, for things bought on credit, and money owed for borrowing to pay for special items, there was not a lot left for them and their families. Many sharecroppers kept track of what they borrowed, rent owed, and any money owed for food bought on credit. There were many who knew they did not owe as much as said. These sharecroppers did not argue with the plantation owners about shortening their names, nor did they disagree with the owners about the amount they said was owed. In those days, Blacks were not allowed to disagree with any white person or white plantation owner about what he said was owed him. The sharecroppers could be put off of the plantation with their whole family and what little they did own could be confiscated for collateral. Or they could be taken out and beaten or killed for disagreeing with a white man. This happened to a sharecropper that Papa and Grandmother heard about. The plantation owner said that the sharecropper owed more than he had borrowed. The sharecropper knew that he had not borrowed and taken up as much on credit as the plantation owner said he did. He argued with the owner about the bill. The owner told him to shut up but when the sharecropper continued to argue with the owner, he slapped the sharecropper in the face. Without thinking, the sharecropper slapped the owner. He had already signed and sealed his death warrant the minute he slapped a white man. He knew that he should have agreed, walked away, and tried to talk to the white man later, but it was too late. The damage had already been done. He ran home and tried to hide. Later on that evening, word got to him that a group of white men were coming during the night to beat him, maybe even kill him and his entire family. Some of the black sharecroppers were able to hide him and his family for several days until the search died down some. My mother said that Grandmother told her that none of the black people would say anything about where this sharecropper and his family were hiding. By night, they were able to slip them to another town and got them on a bus going north. They were able to safely escape the mob. Grandmother told Mother no one ever heard from them again as far as she knew.

Mother also told me another story about a sharecropper that Grandmother and Papa knew who had 11 children who were very hard working people. They never missed a day in the field unless it rained or there was a storm. After all of the hard work of hoeing the cotton, gathering the cotton and corn, paying the rent, clearing the debts of everything borrowed and bought on credit, the sharecropper cleared only a nickel. The plantation owner pulled out his ledger, showed the sharecropper his debts owed to the store. After going over the records with the sharecropper, he showed him why he had profited only a nickel for all of the hard work he and his family had done. Even though slavery was not legal anymore, working so hard for a year to get out of debt, only to make one shiny nickel felt like reliving slavery all over again. The only differences now was one could freely come and go without permission and was expected to be paid fairly for their work. If a person in those days did not have enough food or clothes to carry them through the winter, people helped them out.

Although this man only cleared a nickel, the other sharecroppers shared food with them that they had put up for the winter. They shared meat with them when they killed hogs, and they gave them clothes that were too small for their own children. No one in those days allowed people to go hungry and without clothes like some people would do today.

Needless to say, in those days it was very difficult for black sharecroppers. Some were bound to the owners because they were always in a position where they had to borrow more money than they were making. This gave them a perpetual death sentence to the plantation owners because they were in more debt than they were worth. There were some sharecroppers, however, who were very thrifty and did not have to borrow a lot against their crops. Papa was one of the few who did not have to borrow much or get much on credit. After gathering his crops, paying his rent for the use of the land, paying the small amount of money borrowed, and paying the small amount for things bought on credit, Papa always made sure he still had enough to buy what he needed. No matter if it was supplies to prepare for his crops the next year or money to buy clothes and shoes for his family, or money to buy food items that could not be grown. Not to mention Papa had a cash reserve to help him get through the winter months as well. He never spent money on unnecessary things. He only spent money on things that they were in dire need of. Mother once said that Papa was so tight with his money that he could save his money and get the skin off of a mosquito for profit and the mosquito would not lose a drop of blood. What she meant by that remark, I never did figure out. All I knew was that Papa was a man that was good with money.

Grandmother played a vital part in helping Papa save and spend his money wisely. She had many words of wisdom. Grandmother was very wise even though she only finished the fourth grade. As a child, I used to hear her say things like, "The man can bring provisions for his family through the front door and the woman can throw them out the back door and he will never be able to provide enough for his family" or "A woman can either make or break a man". I did not understand what she meant until I was grown and married. What she was saying was that a man could provide for his family but if the woman did not use what he had provided wisely, no matter how hard he worked or how much he provided, it would never be enough for the family. She also taught us the value of a man. Grandmother used to say if a woman did not show appreciation for what her husband had provided and complained all of the time about what he had not done, she could destroy him by making him feel that he was useless and less than a man when he had been doing the best he could for his family.

Grandmother was surely a woman who did not waste anything. She used the money wisely that Papa gave her to buy things needed for the house and the children. She helped Papa by making sure that the garden was planted with all kinds of vegetables. She not only had a large garden with a plethora of choices for produce, but she made sure that they had a "truck patch". Truck patches were part of the land that was used for planting food away from the house. Papa did not have a truck nor could he afford one to transport the food items from the truck patch to the house or anywhere else, but he could use his mules and wagon to bring the items to the house which served just as well as a truck and was inexpensive. Truck patches were much larger than the garden which was close to the house. Truck patches contained a variety of produce like peas, tomatoes, eggplants, okra, collard greens, mustard greens, turnip greens, cabbage, kale, spinach, swish chard, pork salad (which grew wild in the garden and was delicious when cooked with scramble eggs and onions) butter beans, lima beans, navy beans, green beans, green peas, sweet potatoes, white potatoes, beets, lettuce, onions, hot peppers, new potatoes, carrots, and any other kind of vegetables that they wanted to plant.

Monday through Friday, Grandmother, Papa, and the children worked in the cotton field, but Saturday was the time to work in their garden and truck patch. The garden and truck patch had to be hoed just like the cotton. Grass had to be kept from growing around the vegetables because it would hinder their growth.

So Saturday morning was the time to hoe the garden and truck patch until the vegetable plants were large enough to survive on their own. Saturday was also the day to wash and clean in the house. In most families, the older girls worked in the house while the boys helped to hoe the garden and truck patch. When the boys finished that work they were not through. Papa always had other things for the boys to do. No one slept late on Saturday. There was too much to do. When the day was over, everyone had to take a bath for Sunday. No baths were taken during the week. The girls had baths first, then the boys.

Sunday was truly the Sabbath and the day for going to church. No one would ever think of washing or hoeing grass on the Sabbath, it was unheard of. It did, however, happen once with a new family that moved into the community. They had gotten their days mixed up and they did not realize that it was Sunday, so they went to the field and began to hoe the cotton. The people in the community were on their way to church. When they saw these people in the field they were shocked and did not know what to do. Finally, one of the deacons of the church went out in the field and told them that it was Sunday. They were truly embarrassed and explained that they had gotten their days mixed up and thought it was Saturday. They had planned to attend church on the next day which they thought was Sunday even though it was actually going to be Monday.

If no one had told them they would have gone to church and found it empty. The new neighbors believed in the Sabbath and believed that it was a day for going to church and to rest. Some of the people in the community laughed and the incident was soon forgotten. Grandmother told her children that if a day of rest was good for God, then it was more than good enough for them. After a day of rest, Monday came and it was time to go back to the cotton field for more hard work.

The gardens grew and it was time to begin gathering the vegetables and canning them for the winter. There were no freezers or refrigerators in those days, so everything had to be cooked and put in jars. Harvesting and preparing the vegetables for canning was a very busy time for my mother and Grandmother. Nothing was wasted because they knew that winter was coming and it was going to be long and cold. So they wanted to make sure that they had canned enough food to carry them through the winter months. Sharecroppers who had plenty of vegetables shared with one another if other sharecroppers' gardens did not do as well.

Papa and Grandmother were always blessed to have a great garden and a great truck patch. Putting up food from the garden and truck patch was a full time job. Grandmother and Mother did not go to the field during this time. This process of preparing food for the winter posed the same arduous task of picking cotton in the sun. When she and Mother began to put up the food, it was early summer and of course the sun was on high and full display! That made using the wood burning stove to cook the vegetables for canning almost unbearable. Not to mention there was no electricity; therefore, no opportunity for a fan in a stationary position unlike you could use in the field. Sometimes Grandmother and Mother would fan themselves with a piece of paper or a piece of cardboard, but they could not do this continuously because they needed to use both hands for working. Even though the wood stove threw off an excruciating heat that when mixed with the natural earthly temperature was unbearable, that did not hinder them because they would rather sweat all day in the summer than starve in the winter. When they started canning, they usually started with the greens, because they were some of the first vegetables ready to be picked, washed, and cooked. They cooked and canned turnip greens, purple top turnip greens, turnip bottoms, slick and curly leaf mustard greens, collard greens, kale, and swish chard. For dinner most days of the week they ate some type of greens. The greens were always bountiful so there was no need to use them sparingly like some of the other vegetables that could only be harvested during the summer.

After the canning of greens it was about mid-summer. The peas were ready to be picked, shelled, cooked, and canned. They began with the purple hull peas. They started picking them off the vines early in the morning and after dinner they sat out in the yard under the shade tree and shelled the peas. They washed them, cooked them with salt pork, and put them in jars. A person may think the luxury of sitting under a shade tree after burning in the hot sun all day provided some sort of relief to the women, but it didn't! That was still a great deal of work.

The next morning they started picking peas again. This was done daily until all of the purple hull peas, crowder peas, field peas, black eye peas, butterbeans, lima beans, green beans (which they called string beans), and green peas (called English peas) were picked, cooked, and canned. This was done over a period of weeks because the vines continued to bear beans and they had to gather them. After they had picked, cooked, and canned all of the peas they wanted and, of course, gave some to the neighbors, the rest were allowed to dry. The dried peas were shelled, put in a flour sack, and hung in the pantry to also be eaten in the winter. Now here's the best part about dried peas - you did not have to cook or wash them until you wanted to eat them.

Next, they gathered the tomatoes, cooked, and then canned them. Some of the tomatoes were used to make vegetable soup. Grandmother would add green beans, corn, okra, and tomatoes together, cook, and can them. This was known as vegetable soup. Mother always said nothing smelled and tasted as good as vegetable soup with cornbread on a cold winter day. The smell of the soup made you feel warm and fuzzy inside. When they finished this, it was approaching fall, but since the weather was still very warm, they went to the truck patch and picked the rest of the dried peas.

After completing these tasks it was time to begin picking and canning the fruits. Some of the fruits were picked and canned earlier in the day, but most of the time was devoted to canning vegetables which were essential to providing all of the healthy nutrients that helped us through the winter months. Now the fruits they picked were apples, peaches, and pears. The interesting thing about the fruits was that they used the peelings and the cores of the fruits to make different kinds of jellies and jams. Peaches were mainly pickled and the other fruits were used more for preserves. Something else they made was watermelon rind preserves. In the summer, when they could find blackberries, they made blackberry jam. Grandmother and my mother dried apples and peaches to be used for making fried apple or peach pies.

The only thing they did not have during the summer months was meat. They did have salted fat meat called "sow belly" because it was the belly of a female hog left from the year before to season the food. It would smell tainted and would be covered with mold after hanging all winter, but it could be washed in baking soda and water to remove the mold and decrease the tainted smell. They used what they had because they knew that winter was coming and they would have fresh meat to eat. Papa had three hogs in a special pen that he was fattening to be killed. The pen was a tall wooden fence with a wood floor so the hogs would not walk in the mud, nor have much room to move about which would allow them exercise, thus causing them to lose weight. In order to fatten them up they were fed corn all the way until it was butchering time.

Two of Mother's brothers, Troy and Jessie, were hard workers like their father. She called them go-getters. She said they never seemed to get tired. Papa could always count on them to follow through on any task they were given. They always went far beyond what they were asked to do. Papa was proud of them. They would see things that needed to be done and they would do them without being asked. Mother said that her brother, Myers, was a different story. He worked hard, only because he knew that he had no other choice. He was not as willing as his brothers to go the extra mile without being told sometimes. Papa was a strong man. He knew that someday his sons were going to marry and have families of their own and they needed to be strong men who would work and provide for their wives and children. Papa could not stand a lazy man so he would not allow his sons and daughters to be lazy people.

As Mother's sister Hannah grew, she became the babysitter for her youngest sister and brother. Now, Mother was able to go to the field with her parents, her three brothers and her little sister, Clare. Aunt Clare came along even though she was small and could not do a whole lot, but she was willing to try. Mother said that she thought Aunt Clare was born independent. She had a mind of her own and she was not a lazy child. Papa now had four able-bodied children in the field and one little helper. Along with he and Grandmother, this made a total of seven people to hoe the cotton. Papa said that he had six helpers with himself and Grandmother, but Aunt Clare would correct him and let him know that she was the seventh person. Papa really did not count her because she was not old enough to hoe a whole row of cotton by herself, but he did not want to discourage her. One of her brothers would help her hoe her row of cotton along with the row they were hoeing. They could hoe at least 35 or more rows of cotton before it was time to leave the field and go home for dinner. When they went back to the field after dinner, they were able to do more rows of cotton than in the morning, because they stayed in the field until well after the sun had set. When they went to the house it was dusk dark, but there was still time to see how to do the evening chores. They were tired, but they did their chores right. They knew that Grandmother and Papa would not allow them to do sloppy work. They did the work hurriedly but correctly. The earlier they got the chores done, the sooner they were able to get a light supper and get ready for bed. They looked forward to a night of rest. The boys slept in one room and the girls slept in another room. They did not have the comforts that we enjoy today. The boys had to share one bed in their room and the girls had to share beds in their rooms. The nights were hot so they slept with the windows open. Sometimes a cool breeze would blow through the opened windows, but often times the breeze that blew through the opened windows was hot.

Mosquitoes were bad in the summertime and so were bed bugs which were really bird lice. The mosquitoes came through the windows and buzzed around their heads driving them crazy as they waited to see when they were going to be bitten. Many nights their rest was interrupted because of these critters. They had to try and fight off the mosquitoes until they finally went to sleep, and then the mosquitoes would feast on them as much as they wanted until they were completely full of the children's blood. Joining the mosquitoes sometimes were the bird lice. They would bite the children and they itched so badly that sometimes it seemed almost unbearable.

Grandmother did not have bird lice because she kept an unclean house. Her house was always clean, but birds would roost on the roof and under the eaves of the house, so the lice came from them. Some people referred to them as bed bugs. Grandmother was not the only person bothered with bird lice. Everyone had problems with lice if birds were roosting on top of their house. There were many people with this same problem. Grandmother would take the mattresses off of the beds, take them out in the sun, pick the lice off, spray the mattresses with disinfectant spray, and let them lie in the sun all day. She then would wash the bed springs with hot water and lye soap. This would kill the lice for a while, but the same procedures had to be repeated until the summer months were over. She and Papa were fighters. They did not allow this problem to defeat them.

Summer was a busy time. Everyone on all of the plantations was very busy. Grandmother would say, "Work while the sun is shining and when winter comes you will not be like the grasshopper, hopping around all summer singing and having a good time, then winter comes and he has nowhere to lay his head, no food to eat and no place to keep warm." Everyone worked very hard and they did the work in hopes of producing great crops and reaping the benefits of their hard work.

Summer had come and gone and fall was slowly fading into winter. The gathering of cotton was finished and all of the corn had been pulled and stored in the barn along with hay for the cows. Through all of the family's efforts, we now had more than enough canned for the winter.

Now it was time to dig up the sweet potatoes, white potatoes, and pull up the peanuts. Everyone could help with this venture. Papa would hitch one of the mules to the plow and plow up the potatoes. The potatoes were gathered and brought up to the house where they were covered with chicken wire and allowed to dry in the sun for a while. While the potatoes were drying, Papa dug two shallow holes. Into the bottom of these holes, he placed old cotton sacks with tar bottoms. Over the cotton sacks he placed old burlap sacks and chicken wire on top. Papa placed the potatoes on top of the wire; sweet potatoes in one hole and white potatoes in another. He covered the potatoes in each hole with a mixture of hay and dirt. The holes were covered with a piece of tin. Whenever potatoes were needed all they had to do was remove the tin and move some of the hay and dirt to get to them. They always had enough potatoes to last all winter. After digging the potatoes and securing them for the winter, it was time to pull up the peanuts. Although this was hard work and not an easy task; it was fun! The reason this was a source of amusement was due to the fact that they could not tell how many peanuts a vine had on them from the surface because the nuts were on the roots of the vines. This left the total number of actual peanuts a mystery until they pulled them up to harvest them. When the vines were pulled up, they were turned upside down so that the sun could dry the peanuts. When they dried, they were picked off of the vines, placed in burlap sacks, and put away for the winter. Here is where the fun kicked in! Papa and the kids would play a guessing game to determine the number of peanuts on the vine. The rule of thumb here was depending on how hard the vine was to retrieve from the ground determined how fruitful the vine was. Sometimes they would pull very hard thinking their vine was full of peanuts, but when the vine came up out of the ground there would only be a few. Once in a while, Grandmother would join in the game. That was plenty of fun because sometimes she would pull with all her strength and there would not even be a half dozen peanuts on the vine. Most of the time she and Papa would be the losers and the children would be the winners. What fun it was to win over their parents. The children could stop pulling up peanuts from time to time and eat some of the green peanuts, but Grandmother did not let them eat too many. Green peanuts could give them diarrhea and diarrhea would kill them. In the winter time when all the chores were done and supper eaten, before going to bed, Grandmother would put a big pan of peanuts in the stove and roast them. Roasted peanuts smelled good when roasting, and they tasted so good on a cold winter night. When the peanuts were through roasting, everyone got a chance to enjoy the warm protein source before an evening of slumber.

Although peanuts were the main type of nuts they also would pick up black walnuts and hickory nuts. This was a very difficult task and did not provide the amusement that peanuts did. In order to get to the meat of the nuts they needed a hammer or something hard to lay the nuts on to crack open the hard shell. Sometimes Grandmother would let them use the bottom of an old smoothing iron no longer used for ironing clothes, but she never let them use her good smoothing irons. If they had no iron to lay the nuts on, they used a brick. Mother said that when cracking these nuts they had to be careful, because sometimes they missed the nut and hit their fingers. When one of them did this and cried out in pain she said that Papa would say, "Felt good didn't it?" The child that had hit his or her finger would laugh and get busy cracking nuts again. Mother said that she remembered these times as some of the happiest times in her life. They were a close knit family and they were not afraid to show that they loved one another and they enjoyed the times they spent together.

As children, Mother and her siblings were not allowed to argue or fight one another. If their parents caught them doing this, they would either get a whipping to their backside or they would have to go and sit by themselves and think about what they had done. Afterward, they had to go and apologize to the one they had an argument with. She said that they got into arguments when no adults were around but they never hit one another. The boys had fun wrestling, boxing, and horsing around as they called it. Mother said horsing around meant throwing rocks, balls, and chasing one another. They never got angry with each other if one did something better than the other. Mother's sisters Hannah and Clare got into arguments. At times she said they got to be heated arguments, but they never hit one another. Mother said that she sometimes felt they were like oil and water, they just did not mix. They each thought that they knew more than the other. Grandmother never knew about these arguments.

When winter finally reached the plantation it did not pull any punches! It was bitterly cold outside and the ground was frozen hard as a piece of granite. It very seldom ever snowed in this part of the country; therefore, the main concern was with ice on the ground. There was no more work to be done in the cotton and corn fields until ground breaking and planting time. Outside work was over but there were the chores to be done outside in the cold. Papa and the boys did the feeding of the chickens and the hogs, gathering and cutting wood, and feeding the cows. Grandmother loved to milk her cows and gather the eggs. She would bring the milk right in after milking the cows, strain it, and set some aside for drinking and cooking. The rest she would put in containers to clobber and make ready for churning. After the churning, they would have butter to eat and buttermilk to drink. Grandmother's family loved the desserts she made. My mother said that Grandmother made the best buttermilk pies, egg custards, egg pies, sweet egg rolls, butter rolls, sweet potato pies, sweet potato cobbler, apple cobbler, peach cobbler, blackberry cobbler, and bread pudding that she had ever eaten in her life. They always had something sweet to eat at dinner time all year round, even when they did not have meat to eat.

As the weather continued to grow colder, it was time to butcher the hogs. Butchering time was done in the latter part of November or early December. Thanksgiving was not celebrated; but they set aside a whole pork shoulder to bake for Christmas dinner.

Preparing for the butchering of the hogs began the night before. Water had to be pumped and put in a big black cast iron wash pot in the backyard. Wood was placed around the pot to be used for starting the fire early the next morning. The water in the pot had to boil so that it would be ready to use when the hogs were butchered.

Earlier in the week, Papa would cut six small, young, strong trees. For the first three trees, he removed the limbs and took an ax and trimmed the bottoms to make sharp points; after which, he cut a square piece from each tree several inches from the top. When this was done, he took the second set of trees and removed the limbs. He cut several inches from each end of the trees and nailed these trees into the squares he had cut in the first set of trees. When he was through with the trees, he took a shovel and dug three holes and placed the sharp points of the trees into the holes and packed dirt around them so that they would not move. These trees were going to be used to hang the hogs on after they had been butchered.

On butchering day everyone was up bright and early. There was so much to be done. Papa did not eat much breakfast on the day that he was going to butcher hogs. He would eat a biscuit with butter and drank black coffee. He did not eat much because of the sight of blood and the smell of the hogs. To be honest, after they had been killed and opened up, he often times became extremely nauseated. But he could not neglect his duties. He had to do what he had to do. On butchering day, a neighbor and Papa's sons butchered the hogs. After butchering the hogs, they were dipped in a barrel of hot water taken from the black cast iron wash pot. They were then taken from the barrel and hung on the trees by the leaders in the hind legs. Sharp knives were used to scrape the hair off of the hogs. After all of the hair was removed, their stomachs were cut open and the hog's internal organs were removed. The livers, hearts, kidneys, and what we called the "lites and melts" were placed in large dish pans and set aside. The large intestines which are called "chitterlings" were removed and placed in a number two tub. There they were cleaned, washed, and brought into the house to be cooked, canned, and eaten when they wanted to have chitterlings for dinner. The small intestines were washed and cleaned also, but they were not eaten. They would be used to stuff sausage in them after the sausage was made. The hogs hung on the trees until they were cool from being dipped into the hot water to remove the hair. The hogs were taken down and laid on make shift tables made of boards placed on wooden quilting horses. They were cut into various cuts such as hams, shoulders, backbones, and "middling meat" known as bacon. Some of the lean scraps of meat cut from the backbones, ribs, hams, shoulders, and middling meat was set aside to be used to make sausage and some would be used later on that day to cook for dinner. Nothing tasted as good as those scraps of meat cooked with onions and gravy served over hot rice or mashed potatoes with biscuits. The food smelled so good while cooking that the anticipation of waiting to eat the food was overwhelming.

Now that the butchering was over, it was time for Grandmother and the girls to begin their work. Preparations were made to make hog head souse. First, the heads, feet, ears, and tails of the hogs were cooked, and the girls helped to remove the bones from the heads, feet, and tails. All of the meat was ground using a manual hand grinder. Next, parched sage leaves were crushed into a powder. Then salt, black pepper, vinegar, red pepper, and a small portion of chopped onions were added to the meat and it all was mixed together to make souse. The souse was packed in several large pans and set aside to jell into hog head souse. Brown paper was cut and placed on top of the souse in each pan and heavy boards were placed on the brown paper to press the souse down. The brown paper also helped to absorb some of the grease from the souse.

Next, it was time to make the sausage. Grandmother took some of the lean meat, ground it with some of the fat from the hogs and added spices, along with other seasonings and made sausage. To preserve the sausage, she stuffed some of it into the small intestines and hung it in the smoke house to smoke until it was cured. Some of the lean meat she cooked and placed in jars to be eaten during the winter. The hams, middling meat, and shoulders were placed in brine made of salt water, liquid smoke, and brown sugar. The meat was taken out of the brine after a few days and rubbed with salt and brown sugar, then hung in the smoke house to be cured. A fire was set in the smoke house and the wood was fixed so that it would not blaze up, but smolder until the meat was cured. The smoldering wood was put out and the meat would remain in the smoke house all winter to be used when needed. There would be either ham with red eye gravy or middling meat or sausage to be eaten for breakfast or dinner. Red eye gravy and ham was an excellent meal. Red eye gravy was made by using some of the grease from the ham and adding black coffee to the grease thus giving it the appropriate name "red eye."

The backbones were cut into smaller bones, seasoned, and cooked. When they were done, my grandmother took sterilized jars and put the meat in them along with some of the liquid. She put the lids on the jars and turned them upside down to seal them. She did the same thing for the ribs. She cooked them, seasoned them, and put them into jars. After making all of the sausage she had some of the scraps of meat left over. Although she had already canned some of the meat, she was not going to let any meat go to waste. In these times people were not wasteful, they found a way to use everything! Grandmother cooked this meat along with the melts, lites, hearts, livers, kidneys, and chopped it into bite size pieces, seasoned, cooked, and put this meat into jars. This was called "hog hash". Hog hash was very good on a cold winter day. It was served with hot cornbread and a vegetable. Almost everything on a hog was used for one thing or another. The hog's hooves were used for medication. The hooves were parched in the oven of the stove and they were crushed into a powder. The powder was put into a glass container and when anyone got sick with a cold, some of the powder was added to hot water, honey, and a small amount of liquor. This was known as "Hog Hoof Tea" used to cure colds.

All of the vegetables, fruits, nuts, and beans had been canned and put away for the winter. The meat was also ready for the winter. Grandmother never sat around idle. She always had something to do. On some days when her work load did not keep her completely busy for that day, she pieced quilts. Mother said that she did not know a time when her mother was not completely busy. She never seemed to have any spare time because even during her spare time she was quilting. She loved to piece quilts. She saved old material and cut it into squares and other designs and sewed them together to make quilts. Grandmother had lots and lots of quilts and every year she made more. Her intent was to give each of her children quilts when they got married and started homes of their own. Some of the quilts she made like the Double Wedding Ring and other fancy designs were not for everyday use. These quilts were used when company came or when some of the relatives came from Kosko for a few days visit.

During a visit, one of Grandmother's sisters came from Kosko, which is referred to as "the hills", because it is very hilly and not flat land like the Delta. She stayed for two weeks. They had loads of fun sitting around the fire talking about their childhood and piecing quilts. Grandmother and her sister both had long hair. During their time no one pressed their hair, and perms were unheard of. They washed their hair, oiled it, and wore it in two braids or some other style. If the hair was not long enough to braid, they had a way of twisting the hair to keep it in place. When they were children, their mother did not have a lot of patience with them when combing their hair. She combed very roughly and if they whimpered while getting their hair combed, their mother would peck them in the head with the comb, and she would continue to peck them until they were silent. They laughed about it, but said that it was not funny when they were children. My mother said that Grandmother did not get to go back to her hometown very often after moving to the Delta, but when she did it was so nice. It was also enjoyable to have family members come for a visit. This made plantation life bearable. This was considered the way of living. In everybody's eyes they were living what they considered the good life. Life always got better at Christmas time!

Chapter 4

CHRISTMAS ON THE PLANTATION: A FAMILY TRADITION

After Grandmother's sister left, it was time to start planning for the Christmas holidays. It is safe to say the amount of attention Papa and Grandmother gave to Christmas in the early 1900's was nowhere near the level of attention nowadays. To be honest, they considered the fact that they had food, shelter, clothes, shoes, and good health as the best Christmas present that anyone could ever desire. Actually, Mother and her brothers, Jessie, Myles, and Troy were made aware at an early age that there was no such thing as Santa Claus. However, they never shared that information with the other children because they did not want to spoil Christmas for them. Even though Papa and Grandmother had added two young children to the family, the older siblings still did not ruin it for them either. To them they thought Santa would bring raisins on the stem, nuts, candy, an apple, orange, and some kind of small toy.

Grandmother began her baking for Christmas at the beginning of December. None of the neighbors exchanged Christmas presents, but they baked cakes and when someone came by on Christmas day, they were given a plate full of the different kinds of cakes for a present. If some of the neighbors whom Grandmother and Papa knew well did not come by on Christmas day, they were sent a plate of cake. The neighbors returned the favor by sending or bringing Grandmother and Papa cake.

Mother, Troy, Myles, Jessie, and Clare were back in school now since there was no field work to be done. Mother could help with the baking when she came home from school. Black children did not go to school for nine months because they had to wait until the crops were gathered before they could go to school. So Mother did not miss any days from school to help at home. She helped cook and did other chores when she got home. Grandmother baked jelly cakes, coconut cakes, chocolate cakes, pound cakes, caramel cakes, lemon cakes, molasses bread, and a very large batch of tea cakes for the children to snack on before Christmas. She always made small samples of her cakes to see how they tasted and if they would rise well. The children got to eat the samples and best of all to lick the bowl and spoon.

It was a certainty that Papa and the boys had to supply a heaping amount of wood for the stove because it would be working around the clock preparing the cakes. Grandmother did not own cake pans so each layer of a cake was baked in cast iron skillets. Only one cake could be made at a time and each cake had three layers. When she finished her Christmas baking, she would have baked over 40 cakes. Then they were placed in a big tin trunk with an oval shaped top waiting to be eaten at Christmas. I laughed when my mother told me about Grandmother baking anywhere from 40 to 45 cakes for Christmas. I could not imagine anyone baking that many cakes, but it was a tradition amongst southern Blacks when Mother was growing up.

Early on Christmas Eve, Papa brought a pork shoulder in from the smoke house. It was washed and placed inside a big pot of water where it was parboiled to remove most of the salt. After parboiling, the shoulder was placed in a roasting pan and placed in the wood burning oven for a nice long cooking session. By early evening, the shoulder was done and it was set on the table along with pies and some of the cakes taken from the trunk to create a festive look. Three large ducks were the last thing to be placed in the oven. It did not take long for ducks to cook. They would be done before night fall.

There were no Christmas decorations nor was there a Christmas tree especially for black people that Mother and her family knew. Mother said that many of the wealthy white people had Christmas trees, but she never got to see them nor did she have any idea of what the decorations looked like.

On Christmas Eve, every one prepared for bed. The smaller children were so excited that it was hard for them to go to sleep. They were told that if Santa Claus came and found them awake, he would put ashes in their eyes, and he would not leave them anything. Children in Mother's family did not put out stockings on Christmas Eve. Each child used his or her shoe box that their winter shoes came in. The shoe boxes were placed by their beds and their presents were placed in them. Everyone was up bright and early on Christmas morning. The older children, Myles, Jessie and Troy knew what they were going to get for Christmas because basically they got the same thing every year - warm underwear, socks, and pants. Mother and the girls got underwear, stockings, and a new dress. Mother's sisters, Hannah and Clare also got some type of small toy. The two youngest children got underwear, clothes, but also got toys like a doll for my Aunt Ava and some kind of toy for our youngest uncle.

Everyone, including the older and younger children, got an apple, orange, raisins, candy, walnuts, and pecans in their shoe boxes. They were happy and thankful for the things they had gotten for Christmas. Mother said that she could not remember what her parents gave each other for Christmas. All she figured was that they were happy because their children were happy.

Christmas morning did not stop the children from completing their daily chores. Once the festivities and opening of the presents had ceased, everything was put aside so that the work could be done. The chores were the same as the daily ones - milk the cows, feed the chicken, gather the eggs if there were any, feed the hogs, chop, and bring plenty of wood in the house. The beds had to be made and floors swept. Every child in the house had something to do. After the work was done, it was time to get ready for breakfast. Christmas breakfast was an old tradition handed down from slavery on Papa's side of the family by the slave master. The breakfast consisted of sliced, cold, pork shoulder, hog head souse, cheese, crackers, sardines, and cake. Papa followed this tradition with his family as his family had while they were slaves on the plantation. They never ate without giving thanks for the food that they were about to eat. Papa always thanked the Lord for keeping them a whole year and not allowing the family chain to be broken. His prayers were sincere and straight from the heart. He knew that it was truly a blessing to have food to eat, be alive and healthy with a roof over their heads, clothes on their backs, shoes on their feet, and a warm place to lay their heads.

As they were eating their breakfast, Papa would tell his children that he always wanted them when they were grown, married, and had children of their own, to always tell them about the Christmas breakfast - what it consisted of and how it was handed down from his parents who were slaves. Papa referred to it as the "Christmas Breakfast Tradition." As far back as he could remember being told by his parents, this Christmas tradition started on the slave plantation in Tennessee where his parents, his three oldest brothers, and several of his sisters were slaves. The slave master taught them to follow this tradition on every Christmas morning because the slave master and his family followed this tradition. It was assumed that the slave master gave the slaves their sardines, cheese, and crackers. The slaves were given pig feet and pig ears when hogs were killed so they were able to make souse and used the piece of shoulder they were given to eat at breakfast and dinner. These items were thought to be their Christmas presents which were given once a year. Mother said she was told that not all of the slave owners did this for their slaves.

When Papa's parents and his siblings were freed from slavery after 1863, they came from the slave plantation to the Natchez Trace in a covered wagon to Kosko. With them they brought this tradition. Papa wanted his children to remember that his father died when he was 11 years old. He wanted them to remember that his mother, father, older brothers, and several sisters were slaves. He wanted this knowledge to be passed down through us - the next generation. Papa wanted his children to remember that he was the youngest of 16 children and that six of his siblings were unaccounted for. It was a possibility that they were sold as slaves before the birth of his three oldest brothers or they could have died at birth. He wanted them to remember that his mother was part Indian, and she came from a plantation somewhere in Virginia, and was sold to the owner of the slave plantation. She was given in marriage to Papa's father. Papa's mother kept the breakfast tradition alive through her children. Papa kept the tradition alive and passed it on to his children. I remember that my mother, grandmother, and Mother's sisters and brothers kept the tradition alive and passed it on to us.

After breakfast was eaten and the history of the breakfast tradition was shared, the adults cleared the dishes from the table, washed them, put them away, and began cooking the side dishes for the Christmas dinner. The cornbread was made for the dressing the day before. Several large jars of vegetables such as peas, okra, and greens were opened and eggs had to be added to squash that was going to be fried with onions. Corn was prepared for cooking. Sweet potatoes were peeled for making candied yams. White potatoes and eggs were boiled for making potato salad. Onions were peeled and cut to be put in the dressing. The egg pies, sweet potato pies, buttermilk pies, egg rolls, biscuit puddings, peach cobblers, and apple cobblers had been made two days before Christmas Eve. In the south, it was customary to eat dinner early. To make this happen, the girls got into the kitchen and helped their mother get everything ready. On top of all the other foods they had, there were the ducks, pork shoulder, and dressing to be added to the feast.

After dinner, the dishes were washed again and the table was cleared of all the food except for some of the cakes and pies. They always had someone to come by on Christmas, if only to say "Merry Christmas!" Those were happy days according to Mother. The evening was concluded by a few visitors from other families on the land. This was a resting time for Papa and Grandmother. They were able to put their feet up and chat with the other adults that stopped by while their kids played with Mother and her siblings. Every one ended the night with a healthy plate of cake or food packed up in a sack. It would be rude to refuse taking a plate of cake from friends. After the Christmas holidays were over, it was time to get back to the daily routine.

Chapter 5

MOTHER WANTED AN EDUCATION

Working as a modern day homemaker and seemingly as half-slaves, an education was not always priority for black children on the plantation. To validate this point even more, black children only went to school six and a half months out of a year if time permitted. If home life or a heavy winter destroyed a lot of crops and more work was needed to prepare for summer, a young child could find themselves working overtime in the field and the classroom was put on hold. School in those days was not in session for nine consecutive months. The months were broken down to four and a half months in the winter, and two months in the summer if the field work was done. Since work was the priority and school was secondary, the schools for black students did not open until the work was done. School usually began the first of October and ended the second week in March. The summer session began in June and ended the first of August. Now when it came to white children who worked in the fields, school was the priority. Regardless of whether the work in the fields was completed or not, white children were able to get all of the time allotted for them to go to school.

This was hard for my mother because she loved school. Mother and her sisters and brothers attended the Woodson School. Mother loved school so much that she fantasized about going to school without interruptions. But since going to school was sporadic she made good use of the time that she did have in school.

While the children were in school, the sharecroppers began plowing and "harrowing" the land during the early spring, getting the ground ready to begin planting their crops. Some sharecroppers kept the older boys out of school to help with the work because there was so much to do to get the land ready for planting. The land had to be broken up with a plow then harrowed. Harrowing the land meant using an agricultural instrument with spike-like teeth or upright disks, drawn chiefly over plowed land to level it, break up clods, root up weeds, etc. The rows had to be built up to plant the cotton and corn. Only one row could be built up at a time. If some sharecroppers did not have help they would never be ready to plant on time.

It was imperative that they got the land ready for planting and got the seeds in the ground. Papa did not like keeping the boys out of school so he normally only kept them out for a week or two just to help with the plowing. Papa could handle the seed planting. Sometimes the boys did have to miss several weeks during the school session because the land had been frozen solid and was slow to thaw which left the land like "marmoreal". If you don't know what that feels like, picture a land of dirt that was hard as a marble counter top.

This only happened a few weeks out of several school sessions and that was okay with Papa, because Grandmother and Papa were only able to finish the fourth grade before they had to quit school and help with the farm work. They considered any school the boys and girls could get was good. Grandmother was a force in making sure Papa got the kids off to school because she wanted her children to have a better education than Papa and herself.

It seemed to Mother that each year followed the same routine, hoe the cotton, pick the cotton, start gathering and putting food up for winter, finish and go to school for the two summer months and enjoy those months of school. After summer school, it was time to gather the cotton before they would be able to go to school again. Mother loved school and she hated when it was over. Grandmother said that Mother had such a craving for learning that she read whatever she could get her hands on. Mother's thirst for knowledge did not just stop at what people would consider normal literary works. No ma'am! She even found herself reading every page of any catalog or magazine she could get her hands on.

Although the children did not have the same passion for education that Mother had, they looked forward to finishing the work that was allotted to them in the field so they could get back to school again. They looked forward to seeing their friends whom they did not see while they were working. School gave the children a chance to interact with their friends, which was a much needed interaction since working on a plantation there normally was no downtime to play with other children. Besides Christmas, there was no time to mingle with friends and other families. Even though there was no time to waste visiting, the children and the adults were able to see each other once a month for church services or sooner if someone in the neighborhood died.

People went to church but they did not waste a lot of time standing around on the church grounds making conversation. Greetings were exchanged because everyone was happy to see each other and to find out how everyone was getting along. After greetings and short conversations were exchanged, everyone went home to have dinner and to rest because Sunday was the only day that they had to rest. They also did not waste time because as sure as there was a Sunday; Monday was coming and that meant another day of work.

Mother loved Mondays, especially the years where it looked like the hoeing of the cotton was almost finished and they would be able to make it to the summer school session on time. Mother always prayed that the Lord would not let it rain because if it rained that meant they would have to wait until the ground dried enough to continue working in the field.

Finally, Grandmother, Papa and the children finished hoeing the cotton. The fields were green and beautiful. The plants looked like fields of green carpet. If they got the right amount of rain and sunshine, Papa knew that he was going to have an excellent crop. It was one of the best that he had since moving to the Delta. This made Papa very happy.

With the finishing of hoeing the cotton, the children were ready to begin another summer session of school. To Mother, the first day of school was the happiest day of her life. On the way to school, it seemed as if her feet wanted to take wings and fly there. A thought kept going through her mind as she walked over to the school, "I am in the seventh grade! I am in the seventh grade and I cannot wait to learn what my teacher is going to teach me!" Mother's teacher for the seventh grade was Mrs. Broaden. She expected all of her students to learn. She did not allow them to waste time being foolish and playing when they should be learning. She believed that time wasted could never be regained.

Finally, Mother and her siblings walked the short distance to school. Children walked to school in the rain, shine, sleet, or snow. They counted it a privilege to be able to go to school. It was not like many of the black children today who have transportation to and from school and also have the opportunity to learn and be anything that their heart's desire. Yet, they do not take the initiative to seize the opportunities afforded them. Many people gave their lives so that many of the black children of today can enjoy a life full of opportunities.

As Mother walked onto the school yard, she began to wave at some of the boys and girls she knew and had not seen since the winter session of school. She talked with her friends and found that four of her very best girlfriends were not returning to school. Some of the boys did not return to school. Three of them were her older brothers. They were helping at home. They were almost grown now.

Her oldest brother Troy was dating one of her good friends and classmate who later became her sister-in-law. Her brother, Myles, was also dating one of her classmates and later married her. Her brother, Jessie did not return to school even though he could have but he wanted to help his father and brothers do the work on the farm. He married later, but did not marry one of Mother's classmates. In later years, he married a young lady who was a classmate of his baby sister and brother.

After meeting and greeting the classmates on the school yard, it was time to go inside and get ready for learning. A lot had to be covered in a short period of time. No time to learn could be wasted. Each mind was geared toward learning, and every minute was used to learn. As one reflects on the statement always used by one of the teachers,

"Use the mind that God gave you, no time to learn will be wasted." Unknowingly, this perhaps could have been a statement closely related to today's United Negro College Fund slogan, *"A mind is a terrible thing to waste*."

Mother knew that she could not waste any of the time she had to learn. She had to get as much as she could in the two months that was afforded her to learn. Because of Mother's hunger for learning, Grandmother felt that one day she could become a teacher. Mother had not decided what she wanted to do, all she knew was she wanted to learn. After finishing the eighth grade one could became a teacher. As for Mother, she had not given any thought to becoming one. She sometimes listened to her two youngest siblings say their alphabets and count from one to ten. The family also helped the younger children say what they called their "ABC's," and their "numbers." They were able to recognize and recite some of the alphabet and numbers. In contrast, most children today learn to sing their alphabets and later learn to recognize and say them. When they are taught to count, they learn to count in segments of one to ten, ten to twenty, etc. until they reach 100.

As summer school continued, Mother became more and more excited. Sometimes Grandmother would say, "Sister", (Sister was my mother's nickname), "Settle down, you are going to make yourself sick if you keep getting this excited about school. You are running around like a chicken with its head cut off." Mother said she laughed at this statement. She knew that she could not possibly be running around like a chicken with its head cut off. She remembered what a chicken looked like when its head was cut off or its neck was broken by taking the chicken by the head and ringing it until the neck broke. The chicken would jump and flutter over the yard until it finally died. Mother was always afraid to kill a chicken. The sight of blood and the chicken jumping with a broken neck or its head completely decapitated from the body made her nauseated. She had a hard time trying to eat the chicken when it was cooked. Grandmother would soothe the situation by telling Mother that they had more than enough chickens and that they had to use some of them for food. If they did not eat some of the chickens, they would not be able to feed them all and some would die because of not getting enough food, and it would be a shame to waste what God had provided for them. This made it easier for Mother to eat the chicken, but it did not make it any easier for her to kill or see the chicken killed. She laughed again and thought "Am I really hopping around like a chicken with its neck broken?"

Mother was making a blackberry pie for Sunday dinner. She thought to herself, "Today is Saturday, tomorrow is Sunday, and the next day is Monday." They were in the third week of the summer school session and Mother thought she would not be able to contain herself if Monday did not hurry up and come. She was wondering what she was going to learn new on Monday. Whatever she learned she knew that it was going to help her in the future.

Finally the waiting was over and it was Monday morning again. Mother and the whole family were up bright and early. There was no such thing as a few get up now and the others get up later. Everyone got up at the same time because everyone had chores to do before going to school. Sometimes when Grandmother was getting breakfast ready for the family, three of mother's sisters helped her to do the work outside of the house. Her sister Aunt Hannah helped to milk the cows. Aunt Clare and their little sister fed the chickens, gathered the eggs, brought them in the house, and all three girls cleaned them with damp rags before putting them away. Sometimes they let their baby sister wipe an egg or two since she was old enough and had just begun to go to school.

At the beginning of spring, a neighbor had given Grandmother some duck eggs, turkey eggs, goose eggs, and guinea eggs. She had set them under several hens and the eggs had hatched. Now, not only did Grandmother have baby chicks, but she had baby ducks, geese, turkeys, and guineas. If she was successful in raising them, she would be able to allow each one of them to lay their own eggs, sit on them until they hatched, and when they were big enough they would have duck, goose, turkey, and guinea meat to eat.

The broth from each of these would make good dressing. The dressing from a goose and a duck was very rich and it could give you an upset stomach if you ate too much of it. They could also have chicken and dumplings. Grandmother made the best chicken and dumplings, and Mother helped her make them. First, they had to kill a hen which was too old to lay eggs anymore then put it in a pot with plenty of water. Next, build a big fire in the wood stove and place the pot on the back eye of the stove to cook slowly until it was done. She would then take flour, place it in a bowl, add water and eggs to it, and form it into a ball of dough. They would form the big ball of dough into at least four small balls, and using a rolling pen, she would roll each ball into a large, very thin sheet of dough. She cut the dough into very small pieces and dropped these pieces into the broth of the chicken. Grandmother would even let Mother drop pieces of dough in the pot. The cut dough would be dropped into the pot a few pieces at a time, stirring after each dropping to keep the pieces from sticking together. She rolled and continued to make dumplings until she and Mother had made as many dumplings as they wanted to make. Nothing tasted better than chicken and dumplings.

Sometimes Grandmother would kill an old rooster and let Mother make dressing. Grandmother never wanted too many roosters among the flock, because the older roosters acted as if they owned the place and tried to kill the younger roosters. So, from time to time an older rooster had to become food for the family when its services were no longer needed.

As Mother walked back to the house after milking the cow, she was very happy about the things they now owned. She hurried to the house to eat breakfast and hurry to school. She and her three sisters were very blessed that they only had a very short distance to walk to school. There were children who had to walk two miles one way to get to school. Believe it or not, they were never late. These children valued an education and counted it a privilege to be able to go to school even though they only had two months during the summer.

When Mother talked about education, she always said that if she had the opportunity to get an education as the children of today have, it's no telling what she would have become. It was always hard for her to understand why some of the children of today would not value the opportunities that were at their disposal. The children do not have to worry about how they are going to get to school and back, because the school buses pick them up - and for some, the buses pick them up in front of their homes or close by. Many of the children would not even have to walk to the bus stop to ride to school.

She also talked about the warm coats and the good shoes that the children today have to wear. She said that the cost of these items would have clothed her entire family when she was growing up. Children have choices now that Mother and her siblings did not have nor did they dream of having when they were growing up. The children are able to go to their closets and choose what they want to wear from the many outfits that they own and can even coordinate them. The money spent on a pair of tennis shoes owned by children today would have bought shoes for several families and there still would have been money left over.

As Mother entered the house with her pail of milk, her sister, Hannah, who had helped her milk the cows had gone ahead because Mother was walking slowly and thinking. Grandmother told her to hurry, strain the milk, and get dressed for school so that she could eat breakfast and not be late for school. Mother was holding up breakfast and everyone was waiting on her. She was so happy that she wanted to start singing and dancing because they were in the third week of summer school, but there was no time to keep rejoicing. She strained the milk and hurried to the room she shared with her sisters who were already dressed, and had combed and braided their hair neatly. Mother dressed hurriedly in a homemade blue flowered skirt, a homemade white blouse, old black shoes (the only pair of everyday shoes she owned), and a pair of white socks. She combed her hair and hurried to the table for breakfast. Grandmother told Mother that she could not be late for breakfast again because Papa had work to do and he did not like waiting for everyone to get seated for breakfast. Mother knew that no matter how excited she was, being late for breakfast would not be tolerated.

The children looked nice and neat in their clothes even though they did not have a lot. The few clothes that they had were divided into two categories: 1) school clothes and 2) Sunday clothes. Mother had five homemade skirts and blouses and four homemade dresses for Sunday. The children's clothes were washed and starched on Saturday and hung on the clotheslines to dry. When the clothes were dry, they were taken off of the clotheslines, brought in the house, sprinkled with water to soften them, and rolled into tight balls to be ironed later on in the afternoon. The reason the clothes had to be sprinkled was because the starch put in them was made of white flour and water. These two ingredients were mixed until they became a smooth paste, then water was added to make a thin liquid. The clothes were dipped into this solution after washing and rinsing them. After the clothes were dried, there was absolutely no way to neatly iron them without sprinkling them and rolling them into tight balls. Without the starch, the clothes would not have looked as neat as they would have with starch.

Ironing these clothes was very hard work. The iron, which was called a smoothing iron in those days, had to be placed on top of the stove or heater until it was very hot, and then it was used to iron the wrinkles out of the clothes. Mother did the majority of the ironing because she was the oldest girl. There were no modern adjustable ironing boards like we have today. Back then, the ironing board was a wide board covered with several old sheets to make a smooth surface to iron on.

Mother could not sit when ironing. She had to stand. She not only ironed her clothes, but she ironed for the whole family. Her father's and brother's clothes were the hardest to iron because they were heavily starched. This was done to make the pants look better, last longer, and to iron creases in the pant legs. Grandmother helped with the ironing when she could, but there was so much to be done on the farm that everybody had something to do from the oldest to the youngest. As for the Sunday clothes, they did not need many because church service were held once a month and that was on the first Sunday of each month. By the time they had worn the outfits allotted for Sunday, one each month, and started over again no one would have remembered that they were wearing the outfit that was worn three months earlier.

Breakfast was eaten and it was time to start walking to school. Since Mother and her sisters lived so much closer to the school than most of the children, they did not have to leave as early as those children who had to walk several miles. They did, however, leave early enough to get to school to have time to talk and for the younger children to have time to play before the starting of class. Each child had his or her own little lunch because there were no cafeterias and Mother and her siblings did not want to lose recess time to go home for lunch. As for Mother and her siblings, it would have only taken less than two minutes to go home for lunch. They wanted to take their lunches and eat with the other children. Mother said their lunches consisted of two homemade biscuits, each with fried salt pork and jelly, a tea cake and sometimes, Grandmother would give them each a baked sweet potato. She wanted the children to have enough to eat so that they would use their time learning instead of wasting time thinking about how hungry they were. After eating, they could go to the pump in the school yard and get a drink of water, and then they could play games until it was time to go back into the building. Mother was 17 years old and she was not concerned about playing. She wanted the older girls who had returned to school to hurry and eat their lunches so that they would have time to continue talking about what had gone on while they were out of school. Mother would look for the older girls each day. Finally, she would see them walking down the road. She stood in the school yard waving at them and when they came into the school yard they always gave each other a hug. They were genuinely happy to see each other. Two of the girls were Mother's future sister-in-laws, Paisley and Annabelle. They were very good friends and their friendship lasted all of their lives.

Mother's sister's (Hannah and Clare) little friends finally arrived and they were also happy to see each other. Because they were younger than the older girls, they talked as they played with each other. Several of the girls, as well as the boys, had bought their little sisters or brothers to school who were attending school for the first time. Mother's little baby sister, Ava, was also attending school for the first time. Some new students were crying because they wanted to go back home, and others were so afraid that they would not say a word. They only gave a blank stare and just stood there. Everyone knew that they would get used to going to school and they would love it. How Ava was going to act was yet to be seen.

Mrs. Broaden, the head teacher, came to the door and rung the bell. It was now time to go into the school building. The first thing to be done was to greet the students and begin the school day with devotion. For devotion, they recited a Bible verse and said the Lord's Prayer in unison, then ended with The Pledge of Allegiance. After this, it was time to register the new students and do roll call. After roll call and registration, the young students were assigned their seats. Then it was time to begin learning because they had only two months of school. There was a lot of work to be done by the two teachers. Mrs. Dillard taught the primer, first, second, third, and fourth grades. Mrs. Broaden taught the fifth, sixth, seventh, and eighth grades. Mrs. Dillard began with the primer grade students first because they were just beginning school.

They were asked to stand, state their names, and recite in unison with the teacher the alphabets and count from one to ten with aid from the teacher. The children were frightened because the other children were watching them, but they would not make fun of them if they made a mistake. This was not allowed. A student could be whipped for making fun of other students who were trying to learn. Corporal punishment was allowed. Mrs. Dillard passed out sheets which contained the alphabets and numbers from one to ten. The students were to trace the alphabet and try to recognize as many letters of the alphabets and numbers as they could. If they recognized three numbers and three letters of the alphabet, they were doing very well for starters. Mrs. Dillard would call on them later in the day to recite again. She moved on to the first, second, third, and fourth grade students. She would listen to them recite their lessons, and they would be given seat work to do at their desk. Each grade would be called on in the afternoon to recite the new lessons.

Mrs. Broaden, who taught grades fifth through eighth, was Mother's idol. She gave the fifth, sixth, seventh, and eighth graders their assignments. All grades began with math, reading, and history. They were to do their math on paper, read the story assigned in their reading book, and review the history assignments to answer the questions in both their reading and history assignments. They would be called on before lunch by grade levels to answer questions asked about their reading and history assignments. As each student's name was called they were asked to go to the blackboard to work the number of problems assigned to them. There was no noise. The only voices heard were the voices of Mrs. Broaden and Mrs. Dillard who were each teaching in their own rooms and the students who were called upon to answer questions. They would have science, spelling, and writing classes after lunch.

The morning of the third week of school went so fast. It was now time to go outside, eat lunch, get water, go to the outside restrooms, and play until recess time was over. Mother and her friends sat on the school steps in the shade and ate their lunches. They talked while they ate. They talked about how hard they had worked in the field, in the gardens, around the house, and how happy they were to get a break by going to school. They each talked about what they hoped to learn, about their little boyfriends, and the girls who did not return to school because they had dropped out to help at home or for some other reasons. They missed them, but there was nothing they could do about the situation but wish them well.

Mother's future sisters-in-law knew they would be back for the winter session to complete their seventh and eighth grade years. They were uncertain as to what they wanted to do beyond the eighth grade. But Mother knew what she wanted to do, but money was the problem for almost everyone. It cost money to go to school beyond their eighth grade year. As Mother and her friends sat talking after finishing their lunch, they each said if there was no money to go on beyond the eighth grade, they would be happy for what they had accomplished. Many of their friends did not get as far in school as they did. During that time, if you finished the eighth grade you were considered to be very successful in school. If you finished the twelfth grade you had a very high status.

The afternoon session of school began after lunch. Each of the grade levels was busy reciting their lessons to their teachers and they were happy when the teachers told them that they had done a good job. Before they knew it, the school day was over and it was time to go home. Assignments were given for the next day, the desks were straightened and any paper or trash on the floor was picked up. Everyone sat quietly until they were told they were dismissed to go home. No one ran from the building. School was so much fun. Everyone but the smaller children hated to leave. Everyone was looking forward to getting their chores done, eating supper, finishing their homework, and getting ready for bed so that they could get up, do their morning chores, get dressed, eat breakfast, and go to school again.

Every day in school was a good day and there was so much to learn. Books were exciting and they contained so much valuable information that stimulated the mind. Many of the books were old used books that had been used by white students, but the children did not care that they were used books. They were more concerned with what was contained between the covers of the books than where the books came from, or even the condition of the books.

At the end of each day, it meant there was one day less that the children had to go to school. It also meant that the summer session of school would soon be over and there would be no more school until the winter session. It also meant that the children would be getting ready to go to the cotton fields to gather the cotton, continue to gather and prepare the vegetables from the garden and truck patch, cook, and can them for the winter months.

Finally, the last day of summer school arrived and it was a sad day for the children. They hated to leave one another, but there was nothing they could do about the situation. They had to gather the crops because the money made from the crops would help them to survive until the crops could be planted and gathered another year. Mother and her friends walked slowly toward home and talked about school, the things they had learned, and how they were looking forward to the winter session of school. When Mother got home, she said goodbye to her friends and walked upon the front porch. When she stepped upon the porch she heard her mother ask the other children (who had arrived home before her), where she was. Mother yelled through the screen door telling her mother that she was on the porch. Grandmother told her that she needed to get in the house, get out of her school clothes, and get ready to do some work. The other children were told to do the same thing.

Mother was thinking as she got undressed and put on her work clothes that at the end of the winter session of school she would be completing the seventh grade and would be promoted to the eighth grade. At the completion of the eighth grade, it would be her last year at the Woodson School. She was happy and then she was sad. The thought of leaving a place where she had been for so long was sort of frightening, but she knew that she could not go forward while looking backward.

While the children were in school, Grandmother had gathered some dried peas from the garden and truck patch. Mother and the girls had to shell the peas and put them in a ten-pound flour sack and hang the sack in the pantry. There were still collard, turnip, mustard, and kale greens, and other vegetables left to be gathered, cleaned, cooked, and canned. They had about two weeks to gather as many of the vegetables as they could before going to the cotton field to begin gathering the cotton. When they started gathering the cotton, they had to wait until Saturday to resume gathering the vegetables. Saturdays were very busy days, because not only were they gathering vegetables, they also had to do the washing and clean the house. Everyone in the house was busy. The boys were busy helping Papa do work around the house. They were helping Papa cut trees while the weather was good, haul them to the house to be cut, stacked, and used for firewood.

The two weeks seemed to fly by and it was Monday, time to go to the field to begin gathering the cotton. Everyone was up bright and early, dressed in their work clothes, and ready to do the usual chores before going to the field. While Papa and the children were doing the chores, Grandmother was in the kitchen getting breakfast ready for the family so that they could eat before going to the field. Gathering the cotton required a heavy breakfast and the same applied to hoeing the cotton. Papa had an excellent crop this year and he needed to gather the crop so none would be lost. Some days when it was not too hot, they would hurry home, eat dinner, and return to the field. After eating, they would not take any time to lie on the floor and take a short nap before returning to the field. The cotton was pretty and white, and the field looked like a field covered with snow. The children were happy and did not mind working because they knew that Papa was going to clear a great deal of money for the family. It took the family two days to pick a bale of cotton. When the bale had been picked, either Papa or one of the boys would hitch the mules to the wagon and carry the bale of cotton to the gin where the cotton went through a process called "ginning". It would separate the seeds from the cotton, and remove any of the pieces of cotton bolls or trash that might have gotten into the cotton while it was being gathered. Then it was compressed into an eight to nine hundred pound bale. The bale was fastened with wide black straps to keep the cotton from coming apart. After this process was completed, the cotton was sold and shipped to the manufacturer that bought it. Papa and the plantation owner kept track of how many bales of cotton were gathered and ginned. Finally, Papa and his family had finished gathering the cotton and it was time to pay the rent and pay any bills owed. Papa and his family were very happy. They had come out on top because they had made an excellent crop. After paying everything, he had more money than he had made since moving to the Delta.

It is now the fall of 1928. School started on time because Papa, his family, and the other sharecroppers had finished gathering the cotton before the beginning of the winter session. Fall faded into winter and it was very cold. All of the vegetables had been prepared for the winter and it was again time to kill the hogs which had been in the fattening pen and get the meat ready for the winter.

Since the winter session of school had started on time, Papa and the boys killed the hogs on Saturday morning. The girls helped to do as much as they could on Saturday, because they did not do any work on Sunday. When Mother and her sisters got home from school in the evening, they could help their mother get the meat ready for the winter. Even their little sister Ava who was five years old could help do some small things, but she was mostly in the way. No one wanted to say this to her, because they wanted her to feel useful. Their baby brother, who was born in December, was the youngest of the ten children. He was too little to know what was going on.

Things went well that school year and as usual, it seemed as if the school term flew by and school was out. Mother was happy because she had been promoted to the eighth grade for the next school term which would begin in the summer. She was also happy that her two best friends, Aunt Paisley and Aunt Annabelle, were promoted and were coming back for the summer term as well as some of the other girls. They were all going to complete the eighth grade together the next school term and then they would see what the future held for them.

Papa saw how excited Mother was about school. Now, it could be said that Papa was from another era, he did not believe in educating women. Actually when Mother was set to start the seventh grade, Papa was skeptical about letting her go to the eighth grade. Remember, Mother's parents had to stop their schooling after the fourth grade to help around the house. This added to the apprehension Papa had towards letting Mother continue to the eighth grade. After thinking about it, Papa did agree to let her go another year to finish the eighth grade, but he felt that this was enough education. He thought that it was time for Mother to devote her time to helping around the house. At her age, she should be helping attend to the gardens, quilting, canning food for the winter, cleaning the house, washing, and doing other duties that would be help to her mother. Mother loved school so much that she helped do these things and still attended school, did her homework, and made good grades without any difficulties. Although Mother saw that there were plenty of girls her age that had dropped out of school to help full time around their houses, she thought this was foolish if no one had forced them to drop out of school. She could not understand why they wanted to follow the same trends of their parents if they could continue their education and make life better for themselves. She did not want to drop out of school, and she certainly did not want to get married and start a family until she had gotten all of the education that her parents could afford to give her. She could think of nothing on earth better than getting an education. She hoped to get married someday and have her own family, but her education came first. So dropping out of school and marriage had never crossed her mind. She had set a goal for herself and she was not thinking about deviating from it.

One day Mother had been out gathering eggs and she came into the house and overheard Papa telling Grandmother that it was about time for her to quit school after finishing the eighth grade. She felt as if her heart had sunk to the bottom of her feet. She did not want to quit school, but she knew that if Papa said that her help was needed around the house full-time she had no other choice but to do what she was told. She knew what she wanted, but the decision about her education now rested in the hands of her father.

Mother's father was born during the time when emphasis was not placed on educating a woman. It was Papa's belief that an education for a woman was a waste of time. He felt that a woman's place was to get married, take care of the home, have children, and help her husband with the farm work. This was a despairing thought because not only did Mother want an education but she was actually ahead of most girls her age because she was an excellent reader, wrote well, and was really good in math. Papa knew this because she helped with adding the pounds of cotton after it had been picked and was able to let him know when he had enough pounds to make a bale of cotton. Grandmother listened attentively to Papa's side of the argument but for the first time in their marriage she would not agree with him. Mother sparked something in Grandmother because the women of Grandmother's era were very submissive to their husband and would not dare stick up for themselves on a matter that their husband disagreed on. It wasn't that they did not have a mind of their own - they did, but they did not go against what their husbands said. The man was the head of the home. Papa saw how adamant Grandmother was about my mother finishing her education and he knew that this was not a war that he was going to win easily. He did, however, know that he would win later because Mother would no longer be able to go to school for free after finishing the eighth grade. He would have to pay for her to go to high school and there would surely not be enough money to pay for her schooling because they were barely making ends meet as it was. Paying for schooling was so far out of the question because now you look at crops and food versus one child's education. Even though Papa knew how unhappy Grandmother and Mother were, he sympathized with them, but farming was a way of life for them and paying for an education was not a priority. Papa knew they had three things working against Mother's desire to go forward with her education: 1) they were poor, 2) they were sharecroppers, and 3) they were black.

This did not deter Mother because she still knew that very few girls were able to continue their education beyond the eighth grade. She had hope because the two female black teachers at Woodson School were an inspiration to her. She knew that if they had found a way to continue their education beyond the eighth grade and were now teachers, she believed that a way would be opened for her.

Mother had no idea how she was going to get the money to continue school. She knew deep down in her heart that Papa did not have the money and he was definitely not going to let her work for anyone else for pay. Besides even if she could have worked for someone else, who would she work for? Everyone that she knew was in the same shape as her parents, What little they had was only enough for themselves and their families, and there was nothing extra. She probably could have worked for some of the white people, but how was she going to do this when all of her help was needed to help her own family survive?

After giving much thought to the situation, Mother finally resigned herself to the fact that she was not going beyond the eighth grade. There was no need to worry about something that no one could do anything about. So she planned to finish eighth grade knowing she had made it four grades further than her parents. She just thanked God for allowing her to make it this far. Mother did not know that her mother was planning and praying for direction as to how she was going to get the money to allow her oldest daughter to continue her schooling. Little did Mother know that Grandmother had to start planning ahead of time to save money in order for her to go away to school. Yes, go away to school! That is why the idea of continuing education for Mother was such a preposterous idea to Papa! Woodson School, the only school for blacks in the area, only went through the eighth grade. More unfortunate was that after finishing the eighth grade Mother would have to go away from home to finish grades nine through twelve. This would cost money because she would have to live away from home. She would need money for room and board, food, and the cost of her books. Mother and her future sisters-in-law all talked about leaving home to go to high school. They talked about leaving Woodson School and leaving Mrs. Dillard and Mrs. Broaden who had been their teachers and mentors since they were old enough to go to school. If there was money for them to go away to school, Aunt Paisley, Mother, and Aunt Annabelle hoped that they would all be able to be roommates. They had always dreamed of this for a long time. Mrs. Broaden had assured them that when it was time to go away to school, she knew several people who took in children who were going to school away from home, and that they would watch over them as if they were their own children.

Grandmother did not know how God was going to make a way for Mother to continue her education, but she knew deep in her heart that He was going to make a way for her to get the money. God had answered so many of her prayers over the years, and she knew that He was not going to fail her now. That's what made Grandmother's faith so strong. Although she was a little woman in stature, she was a powerful praying woman full of faith who saw how Mother loved to learn and how her desire to continue learning could not be quenched. She knew that God saw the same thing that she had seen and more, and that he was going to make a way somehow. She lived by faith daily. She used to say that your walk in life is not by what you see, it is by believing in God and that you will receive what you have asked although you do not see it.

If the money could be provided to pay for her high school education, she would be attending a high school which was only six miles from her home. The six miles was like a hundred miles to a person who had no transportation to travel back and forth from her home to her school. So, Mother would have to find boarding away from home. There were other things to think about other than the money to attend school and to pay for boarding. Who would Mother live with? Would she live with a good family who would look after her? How far would she have to walk to get to and from school? All of these things had to be taken into consideration. Mother was seventeen years old and after finishing the eighth grade the next school year, she would be living away from her parents for the first time in her life and they would not be around to give her guidance. Not to mention there were no telephones for blacks in those days, so there would be no way to contact her parents unless she wrote them a letter, mailed it, and waited for them to answer it.

Chapter 6

GRANDMOTHER'S PLAN TO GET MOTHER OFF THE PLANTATION

One morning Grandmother was in the kitchen cooking breakfast when she heard a voice out of the clear blue that said, "Start selling eggs and put some of the money away for your daughter's education. You have more eggs than you need and what about the butter? You have several cows and you have more butter than you need. You can sell some of the butter and eggs." Grandmother said that she knew that was the voice of God speaking to her and He had opened a door. The next morning Grandmother gathered the eggs, and with the eggs gathered she had more than six dozen. She took the eggs gathered in the morning, wiped them with a damp cloth, and placed them under several pieces of thin processed cotton to keep them from breaking. She gathered the evening eggs and did the same thing. She now had more than seven dozen eggs. The following morning she put a small sign on a piece of cardboard box, nailed it to a stick, and placed it near the road. It read, "Fresh Country Eggs for Sale." For three days she sold no eggs. But then on the fourth day a black woman who cooked for one of the wealthy white families that lived in town was on her way to work and saw the sign. She stopped and bought three dozen eggs for the white lady she was working for. This was the beginning of the sale of eggs, and the beginning of making and saving money for Mother's high school education.

Soon word got around that there were fresh eggs for sale out in the country. Cooks began to buy eggs for the white families they worked for. Papa was happy about the sale of the eggs until he found out that all of the money would not be used for the expenses of the house, but most of it would be put away for Mother's education. As Papa stood looking out over the fields lost in his own thoughts, he knew that he had to keep his thoughts concerning his daughter's education to himself. He knew that Grandmother's mind was made up and there was no need to try to change it. One thing he felt for sure and knew was that his daughter would not like being away from home. She had never lived away from home before and he knew after a while she would get over what he called nonsense. Since she was the oldest daughter, she would come on back home where she would be help to the family in the field, as well as helping her mother with the many chores around the house. A farmer needed all of the help he could get and a farmer's life was a busy life. Each season of the year demanded its own work.

As Papa continued to stand there thinking about Mother leaving, he knew that he had to stop thinking about that. She would be home two more years before leaving. If the truth were told, Papa was more worried about Mother leaving home than he was about the money needed to send her to school. Girls just did not leave home to go out on their own for any reason. When most girls left home, they were married and were leaving with their husbands to start a home of their own. Papa knew that he needed to stop thinking and turn his attention to his farming and providing for his family. He had to chuckle to himself and wonder why he was getting all worked up about something that was yet to come.

Before they knew it, it was time for the summer session of school to start. Time passed so fast and before they knew it was the end of the summer session. Seemingly in the blink of an eye, it was time for the winter session to begin. The winter session ended in March of 1929. The eighth grade graduation ceremonies were beautiful. They had finally made it, and each of the eighth grade girls were excited and looked forward to attending high school six miles away. Mother and her best friends Aunt Paisley and Aunt Annabelle finished the eighth grade on March 23, 1929. Mother was 18 years old when she finished the eighth grade. I never learned why she was as old as she was. Those who were ending their education after graduating from the eighth grade were happy that they had the opportunity to get this far in school. For once, those attending high school would be able to complete training at an approved high school. They knew that it was going to be hard since at the completion of the 12th grade they had a major test to pass before graduating. As Mother and her friends left the school, they talked about getting their clothes ready for high school in the fall. When they were a short distance from the school, they turned and looked back at the school. They wanted to cry because they had spent some fun times at the Woodson School. Little did they know as they walked away and looked back at their alma mater that their world was about to drop out from underneath them and that their plans for high school would be shattered like broken glass for many and delayed for others.

The plowing, planting, then the hoeing and gathering of the crops began again in 1929. Mother heard her parents and other adults talking about the economy and that it did not look good; but she was not concerned. Her thoughts were mainly on getting ready to go away to school in the fall. The crops in 1929 did not do well. Papa did not get many bales of cotton to the acre as he had done in previous years. Things did not look good at all financially. Papa had to borrow a little more money than before and he had to take up a little more on credit. Mother felt in her spirit that she was not going to be able to start high school in the fall but no one had said anything to her about the situation, so she decided to keep quiet and wait until something was said.

Late one evening after all of the evening chores were completed, supper had been eaten, and everyone was sitting on the front porch resting and talking before going to bed, Grandmother told Mother that there was something that she and Papa needed to talk to her about. She had a feeling that it was about her going to school, and it definitely was. Grandmother said that she knew all of the older children knew the crops were not good and she had to use the money that she had been saving for Mother to go to school. Mother was sad, but she loved her parents and she would do anything for them. They told Mother not to lose faith, but hopefully next year would be better and she would be able to go away to complete her high school education. They talked about ways of saving money for her schooling. Mother's three older brothers were willing to help in any way they could so that she could go to high school. However, Mother said that she realized later that it was not God's Will for her to go to school that year.

CHAPTER 7

THE CRASH OF DREAMS

People talked about how well they had done financially during the early 1920's, but now they had seen things slowly begin to change. People constantly talked about the changes in the economy, but Mother was not worried because her parents did not seem to be worried. Nevertheless, she found out later how a country could be affected by the loss of jobs and money. Times were to be harder than she had ever known.

Papa went to town and he came back and told Grandmother that some of the whites in town were talking about the Stock Market and they seemed worried. Papa did not know anything about stocks and the Stock Market so he felt that there was nothing for him to worry about. Within months, the whole nation was turned upside down. On October 29, 1929, the Stock Market crashed and it was a dark day for America. Many investors were so distraught that some leaped from tall buildings to their death, some swallowed poison, and some asphyxiated themselves. Thousands upon thousands of people were stunned beyond belief. This economic collapse not only affected America, but it affected other industrial countries. Because of the effect it had on America and other countries, this economic collapse became known as the Great Depression.

As Mother talked to me about the Great Depression, she said that she would never forget that time and the fear shown on the faces of many adults. Her mother and father were very concerned because of not knowing what the future held for poor working farmers, but they never seemed to be worried. That was the first time in her life that she had seen her parents become that concerned about any situation without being worried, and if they were worried, they did not show it.

Grandmother and Papa always told the children that everything was going to be all right. Mother said she remembered when the Stock Market crashed on October 29, 1929. This day was to become known in American history as "Black Tuesday." Banks failed, people lost all of their money, businesses were wiped out, people found themselves without jobs, homes, and even food. It was like a domino effect. It was extremely hard on those people who had a lot of money, and in many cases had more than they could spend in a lifetime. They had been used to living in the lap of luxury. Then within the blink of an eye, everything was gone. Papa's crops had been poor, but they had plenty of vegetables, chickens, geese, ducks, turkeys, and hogs to kill for meat. This particular year, they were also going to kill a calf for meat. There was no money that would amount to much, but they had plenty of food canned and plenty of meat so they would not starve.

Papa continued to go to town occasionally and he would hear what was going on in the world. They did not get very much information since they lived out in the country and they did not have access to a newspaper. Papa also went to town when he had to take care of business. When that was done he could talk to some of the white people who would talk to him about what was going on in the world. Papa was highly respected by many whites in his hometown.

If anyone in town had not known him, Papa could have easily passed for white. There were some whites, however, who did not talk to blacks about what was going on. You also had those who did not mind talking about what was going on in their families and how the depression was affecting their lives. They did not care about blacks or anyone else knowing about their troubles. Other times, Papa was able to overhear some conversations while he was shopping in town.

Papa did not stand around and listen to the conversations of the whites, as some of the blacks did. As he conducted his business, he could not help but over hear what some of them were saying. He knew that what was happening affected whites as well as blacks. He knew that the Great Depression affected some whites more than other whites. Some were used to having more than others and certainly more than blacks. Now don't think that every white person wanted blacks to hear about their troubles. There were still prejudices in the midst of crisis. Some whites would stop talking when a black person approached, waited until they passed by, and was out of hearing distance before continuing to talk.

Mother said Papa always had an old saying that he would often say from time to time when things got tough, "Everybody is in the same boat, and we are all trying to make it up the river without a paddle." Mother said their parents told them that this was no time to look down on anyone else because no one knew what the future held or what was going to happen.

As Papa continued to go to town during the Great Depression, sometimes he would return without any news. Other times he would return with some news stating that there were no changes in the situation. However, he would always tell the children that they had nothing to worry about. Grandmother would add that the Lord will take care of His children and He will provide all of our needs.

Between the years of 1929 to 1932, the economy grew worse and worse. Mother had no idea when she would be able to start her high school education. At this point in her life, she was not worried about her education. She was just grateful that they had food, shelter, and clothes on their backs.

Papa continued to farm, but there were so many adversities to contend with that he had no control over them. Drought and the lack of rain took its toll on the farmers, causing the cotton and corn to not produce as it had in previous years. Insects got into the bolls of cotton and destroyed a lot of the crops. Many sharecroppers were left with no money to buy food and clothes for their families, nor money to pay the rent on the land they rented.

Papa, Grandmother, and their children were blessed. They could not help pay any of their neighbor's rent; but they could and did share food that they had grown in their gardens with some of them. They were blessed that they could extend a helping hand to their neighbors through sharing. Papa and Grandmother said that they would never standby and see their neighbors suffer from the lack of food when they were blessed to have good gardens even when the crops were poor. Neighbors seemed to grow closer to each other during these times of crises. They got together with one another at church and they even had dinners from time to time at the church which they called "having dinner on the grounds". According to Mother, the smaller children on the plantations were still attending school. To help build up the spirits of the children and even the parents, the people in the community along with the teachers would sometimes have some type of program such as funny skits or plays put on by the children. The parents would help and everyone, whether they had children or not, were able to attend. For a few hours this took their minds off of their troubles. Everyone was able to laugh and talk with each other. It was just good to get together. During this time their troubles seemed to flee for a while.

When Papa was troubled, he would always walk with his hands behind him, and he would be in deep thought. Grandmother, Mother, and her sisters and brothers watched Papa for a long time one evening walking with his hands behind him. He was in no hurry and he seemed to be going nowhere. He was just walking and thinking. When he finally came into the house, Grandmother asked him what he was thinking about. He told her that he knew he had to try to find some kind of job to keep the family afloat. He did not know what he was going to do. It was 1933, they had endured four years of the Great Depression and there was no end in sight. Trying to find a job was going to be like trying to find a needle in a haystack. The newspaper stated that the nation was at its worst point in American history. More than 15 million Americans were without work. Papa was a firm believer that one could not sit around waiting for handouts from someone else. He believed that God helped those who tried to help themselves.

After entering the house and sitting silent for a while, Papa and Grandmother began to talk about the Great Depression and reflected on the years after moving to the Delta. They had moved to the Delta in the early 1920's and they had fared very well during the early years. They had been able to make good crops, pay rent, buy clothes for the children, buy food items that could not be raised and were able to save a small amount of money. Many of the friends whom they had met in the Delta had also done well.

In the early years of the 1920's, the future did not look bad at all. As a matter of fact, the future looked bright and promising. As they continued to reminisce, they recalled that the newspapers had stated that prior to the Great Depression, Americans had prospered and they believed that they would continue to be successful in the years to come. A Republican, had been elected President of the United States of America, and as the newspaper stated, he felt that the American people were faring very well. According to the news in his acceptance speech for the Republican Party nomination for the U.S. President, he was quoted as saying, "The American people are doing so well that we are closer to defeating poverty than ever before in the history of any land."

Some of the American people were very excited about their future and so much so, that many of those who had money to invest were busily investing in the Stock Market. New investors were jumping on the boat of prosperity with their rich counterparts, eagerly investing money. In their minds, they believed that they were going to become rich from all of their investments. They also believed that they would become even richer than they already were. People seemed to have gone overboard by placing emphasis on getting rich and enjoying all of the new ideas and new inventions. I guess one could say that they had gone out of their minds with the enthusiasm of getting rich or richer and enjoying their many successes.

During the years of investing, these American people had no foresight or even forethought of what was lurking ahead. After all of the investing and all of the dreams of new investors intending to become rich, and the rich becoming richer, the dreams did not last long. The Stock Market crashed and so did the dreams of the investors. They lost everything and they were devastated. How were they to know that this was going to happen and that their lives would be changed forever? Many wondered how this could have happened. To the knowledge of many, this was the worst thing that had happened in this country and had lasted longer than any other thing that they could remember. The Great Depression had begun in 1929 and was continuing. No one knew that it would go on until the 1940's.

As the economy continued downward, more people lost their jobs. Men, who had once donned expensive suits, ties, and shoes, enter luxurious workplaces, able to spend as lavishly as desired, were now standing in soup lines. To some it was like a bad dream hidden in the midst of darkness and they wished desperately to awaken and find that this was not happening to them. Behind this so called dream was the fact that this was not a dream at all, it was reality. The years ahead were going to be difficult, and the frightening thing about this situation was no one knew what was going to happen. The unknown has always been and continues to be frightening in any situation.

Everyone suffered from the Great Depression. Some of the rich people, who had money in the banks and did not do any investing, hurriedly withdrew their money and were not spending any of it.

The farmers, who produced food products, cotton, corn, and other needed items to keep the nation going, suffered greatly. Farmers who once utilized all of their land were now urged to plant less so that the prices of the products would go up. No one had any money, so no one could afford to buy all of the products that were grown to sell. With there being a shortage of products and high prices for the products that were grown, only a precious few were buying the products. No one believed that there was a need to attribute the shortage and high prices to supply and demand. There was a shortage of products because the farmers could not utilize all of their land. Yes, there were high prices, but certainly no demand for the products when only a few people were able to buy them.

Because the plantation owners were not renting all of their land to the sharecroppers, this affected Papa and his family as well as other sharecroppers. They did not stop farming, but they planted less. Many plantation owners became more and more despondent because they were unable to rent all of their land and were unable to grow and sell their products for cash to pay their mortgages. Many of them lost their farms. Everything was going wrong. When the bottom is falling out of a situation, some people have to have someone to blame for the things that are happening in their lives. Who better than the President of the USA? He became the most hated man in America. The American people were upset with him because they knew that he had to be aware of and knew better than anyone else what was going on in the nation. The question was constantly asked, "Why isn't he doing something about what is going on?" and "Why is he not fixing the problem?" Many thought that since he was a wealthy man prior to becoming President, the situation was not affecting him; therefore, he could not identify with their plight.

Yes, the President of this nation was a rich man prior to becoming President, but he worked hard to get where he was. He owned some lucrative businesses. Papa as well as other blacks and white people listened a great deal to the white plantation owners who were knowledgeable of the political system and kept abreast of everything pertaining to the President and the economy during the Great Depression. Papa often heard the people in town say that if a man could undertake several endeavors and successfully complete them with little or no help, then why was he not helping the people who had voted him into office as President? These people who had put him into office were now starving. They continuously asked, "Why is he not making things right?" He had to do something now! Jobs were lost, businesses were lost, money was lost, stocks and bonds were lost. It was really time for him to rescue this nation and its people. It was time to restore America to her greatness among the nations and help to build the economy so that the American people could again enjoy the American dream. Papa said that whenever he talked to anyone in town, the conversation of the people always seemed to revert to the fact that the President was rich and he had not lost anything. If he did, they did not know anything about it.

The ones who seemed to know everything about the President had not talked about him not being born rich. He was born poor, but he did not allow being poor to hinder him. As the old adage goes, it could be said that He "pulled himself up by his own boot straps" with a bit of help from his uncle.

Papa said that some people said that the President did not have any parents. That was not true. When you enter politics one has to be ready because there are many speculations. Your life becomes an open book. Searching for anything on the candidate begins from the womb to the grave and beyond. He did have parents. But they died when he was young. His father died some time later. Then his mother died leaving behind three young children – the President, his brother, and his sister. He was brought up as a Quaker and taught a sense of humility, along with responsibility. As small children he and his siblings became orphans after the death of their parents and none of the relatives wanted to take all three children so they were separated and sent to live with different relatives. No one seemed to know whether the children continued to live in the same town, if they went to other towns with the family member who took them, or even if they visited each other again while they were children.

The child who would become President of the United States in later years went to live with an uncle. His uncle believed in hard work and he worked Hoover hard, but he was not cruel to him. His uncle was a country doctor. Being an educated man, one would assume that he wanted the very best for his nephew. Maybe his uncle wanted to inspire him to become a doctor or just get an education. Evidently it did not work because his nephew dropped out of high school. No one seemed to know why. He went to work at some type of business owned by his uncle, but this was not his destiny. While working for his uncle, he had the opportunity to talk to an engineer. After talking to this individual and learning the opportunities that were available in the field of engineering, he found that he might be interested in learning more about engineering, and would possibly like to become an engineer.

Now remember, here is a young man who has dropped out of school, and does not have a high school education. How was he going to get into anyone's college without a high school education? He needed to finish high school in order to get into college to study engineering. This situation was soon corrected with the help of his uncle and a tutor. His tutor was able to instruct him in the areas he needed to pass the entrance exam. He was able to take and pass the entrance exam to get into college. Mother said that Papa never heard what grade he was in when he dropped out of high school. When he started college, he did not go to a Quaker college even though he was brought up as a Quaker. He went to the University of Stanford.

After entering college and learning all he could about the different areas of engineering he decided to study geology. He thought that he might like to become a mining engineer. Unlike the students at the university who had their studies as well as a social life, this young man did not have time to have a social life. He had to work part-time to pay for his room and board. It seems like his uncle would have helped so that he could have had some type of social life, but evidently he wanted his nephew to be independent. In the summer time, he was able to find a job which further enhanced his interest in engineering. Since he had to work so hard to pay for his education, and had no social life, people did not understand him. They thought that he was cold and unconcerned about others around him, but this was not true. He just did not have the time to have a social life like some of the students whose parents were probably able to pay for their children's education. His circumstances did not interfere with his making good grades. Children today would have referred to him as a "nerd," but if you look around these are the people who hold most of the top positions in the majority of the big industries.

While in school, he met and fell in love with the only girl in his geology class. This was possibly an awkward situation during this period of time - a girl in a class filled with men. Women usually remained in the background. She must have been a strong woman. She must have had to encounter and endure many criticisms from men, but evidently she withstood the test. Papa said that he never heard any of the whites say whether she got a degree in this area. Because of Papa's belief in educating women, he thought that she was out of her place as a woman and so did a number of other men that he knew, both white and black.

I don't know the number of men who felt like Papa about a woman getting an education, but he really felt that educating a woman was a waste of time. However, it did not change the fact that women were being educated. This young man planned to marry his fiancé after finishing college and getting a job to make money to take care of a wife and children when and if they had any. He did get a job, but it was not in mining. He did not become discouraged - he persevered. His goal was to become a mining engineer. He had a made up mind and an iron clad determination to succeed. He worked some odd jobs until one day his big chance came while he was working in a mine out West. It was said that he worked hard at anything he did. While working in this part of the country, someone recommended him for a job in an English mining firm. This was the beginning of the opening of doors in his favor and the start of his climbing the ladder of success. He was now able to marry his college sweetheart and did on February 10, 1899. Later, she gave birth to their two sons. The children's mother and father were working in China for a while, when some type of trouble began, but they came out safely. Papa did not find out what the trouble was. Mother said that Papa could have probably found out what happened if he stopped to listen to what some of the white farmers said, but no blacks in their right mind would have gone over and stopped to listen to what the white farmers were talking about if they were not talking directly to them. The new engineer decided to leave China and return to the firm in England which gave him his big chance to become a mining engineer and where he became part owner of this business. Being part owner of the mine afforded him the opportunity to get out of the office and the freedom to explore more mines. He was dedicated to his job. He even eventually owned mining companies in America and some foreign countries. Seemingly, everything he was given to do, he did it successfully and he wanted to be in control of everything he did without a lot of input from others.

After he had successfully succeeded as a mining engineer, and his mining businesses had grown astronomically, he wanted to do something different. He wanted to get into politics. This would be a new adventure for him. When you are ambitious and have mastered goals you set for yourself, you sometimes need to set higher goals to work toward. After giving much thought to going into politics and making sure that this was what he wanted to do, he entrusted his businesses to a person whom he trusted would carry on the work and daily operations as he would. Seemingly, everything that he did was successful. He was successful in mining and he was successful in the projects that he was given to do. In each of the projects he was able to show his leadership ability.

The nation had taken notice of his success and leadership ability. So, when Calvin Coolidge did not run for a second term as U.S. President, the Republican Party looked to Hoover as their candidate. Because of his many experiences and successes, he was the one more than likely to become President. He was nominated as the Republican Party's candidate for President and won the presidency in 1928. Hoover became the 31st President of the United States of America.

The next year, October 29, 1929, known as "Black Tuesday," the Stock Market failed and the bottom fell out of everything. Many of the people had not been careful with the spending of their money. They were having a good time. They bought stocks, they sold stocks; but they did not save any money. The money made from buying and selling stocks was too good to miss out on. So, when the money was gone, the President was blamed for the failure of the economy. Although this 31st President may have left the office as the most unpopular President, he really was a success in many areas of his life. Here was an orphan, poor, separated from his siblings, raised by an uncle, became interested in becoming a mining engineer even though he was a high school dropout, tutored to pass the entrance test to get into college, studied geology, worked to pay his tuition, had no social life, graduated from college, finally got his dream job working as a mining engineer, started his own mining companies, and later became the 31st President of this nation - the highest position in the nation. Is there a possibility that this could happen anywhere else other than in this Country? He proved that if you get an education, work hard, and believe in God and yourself, you will succeed. You may not reap the harvest right away, but you should not give up because in due time you will accomplish your goals just as the 31st President was able to do.

This belief could also be applied to my mother's life. She believed that she would be able to continue with her education, but she did not know when this would happen. She did know that she could not give up on her dream. She believed that God was on her side, she believed that her parents would somehow help her to go on to high school, and that this situation, the Great Depression, would not last forever.

The solution to Mother's dream was about to begin. In 1932, Franklin Delano Roosevelt, a Democrat, became President of the United States of

America. He had a lot to contend with coming into office as a newly elected President. The unemployment rate was still high, the economy was very bad, The United States was in a total mess, but it was the new President's intention to get the people back to work. It was not going to be easy. At the time of the 31st President, Hoover had several slogans. One of his slogans was "A vote for prosperity." People thought that he used the slogan, "A chicken in every pot", but that was a slogan of the Republican National Committee. Roosevelt, the newly elected President's slogan was, "A New Deal". He knew that jobs had to be created. If people had money, they would spend it and that would strengthen the economy.

While trying to get America back on her feet, he was faced with the effects of World War II, the bombing of Pearl Harbor, along with other disasters. He was determined to get the American people back to work - and he did. With the creation of jobs, the Depression did not go away all at once. He created a number of New Deal Programs to save the American people.

Through one of these programs, The Works Progress Administration Act, Papa and two of his older sons were able to get jobs. This program was created to hire the unemployed to build buildings, bridges, and miles of roads. The supervisor who hired Papa to help build roads could not hire Papa's two older sons, Myles and Troy, but he had another supervisor to hire them. Mother said she thought they were making a dollar a day for a full day of work which did not sound like much, but it was a lot in those days. At the end of the week, they were able to bring home $15 dollars. Along with what they were making from farming and the amount they made working, they were able to keep their heads above water. Grandmother was still planting her garden and truck patch. She was still canning food and preparing delicious meals from the vegetables in the garden and truck patch.

The money that Papa and his sons were making would help Mother to go on with her education in the future. No specific date had been set because no one knew what was going to happen, but Grandmother would put aside a small amount of money as often as she could. Papa and his family continued to do as well as one could do in those days. Mother continued to hold on to her dream of attending high school in the near future.

CHAPTER 8

MOTHER MOVES OUT AND ON

In the fall of 1932, three years after finishing the eighth grade at the age of eighteen, Mother was able to go to high school. Grandmother put aside a little money each week. They also sold a young cow known as a "heifer" to help defray the cost of her schooling. Mother did well in school because she loved school and she loved learning new things. In 1936, at the age of 25, she finished her high school education. Mother received a Provisional Elementary License from the Department of Public Education authorizing her to teach in the public schools of the state she resided.

Mother said that this was a glorious day in her life. She was now able to teach and she could be some help to her parents for all of the things they had done for her and the things that they had done without so that her dream could be fulfilled. She said she knew that Papa was happy for her, but she could not remember him congratulating her for a job which she thought was well done. Her mother on the other hand, was very proud of her and told her often how happy she was that she had finished her training and was now a teacher.

In the fall of 1936, my mother got her first teaching assignment. She taught the third graders. She rented a room from my father's mother. She said that at the time she rented the room she did not know my father. He had been married and had two children by his first wife. When Mother met my father, he and his wife were divorced and she moved away with their children. Mother finished her first year of teaching and in the fall of 1937, began teaching in another town. There she met my father. He explained to her that he had been married, was divorced, and had two children. Mother did not mention whether or not he had to pay child support. She said that he seemed like a nice man. After they started dating in 1940, she said that he was a very nice man. So when he asked her to marry him, she did. Both of my parents were employed. My father did carpentry work and my mother continued to teach.

At the end of 1941, my father could not find any carpentry work so he and my mother moved near her parent's home. They rented from a white plantation owner, who rented farm land to people wanting to farm. At the time of their move, Mother gave up teaching because there were no teaching positions available for new teachers. In March of 1942, my mother was pregnant with me, her only daughter. She gave birth to me in December of 1942. People always said that I was born in the red house on the highway. When I was about three years old and could understand some things, I wondered how I could have been born on the highway and no cars or trucks had run over me. It was true I was born in a red house, but it was *not* on the highway, it was located near the highway. After making two poor crops my father decided to move back to his hometown and start looking for carpentry work again.

He did move back to his hometown and did find work. As a matter of fact, he found an excellent job which afforded him with more work than he alone could handle. I was three years old when my parents moved back to my father's hometown. After the move, my mother became pregnant with my brother. My father was working long hours and he was making a lot of money. He would bring his money home, and he and Mother paid the bills, bought food for the family, and some of the other things that the family needed. Mother would go to the bank and put the extra money in their account. My father always said that he did not need any money for himself, but Mother would insist that he take a few dollars to have as pocket money.

Mother was so happy. She knew that with the money being made she could make a comfortable home for father, herself, and their children. My father continued with his work and my mother with being a housewife. Mother did not miss teaching school because each day was full of excitement and plenty to do around the house. I had to be taken care of and she was expecting a baby so her mind was on taking care of my father, me, the baby she was expecting, cooking, washing, and ironing. The days went by so fast. Mother loved spending time with our father after work and being able to sit and eat dinner as a family. Often time she found herself thinking of what a blessed woman she was to have a husband who did not mind working and loved her and their children.

I remember one morning my mother was not in the kitchen getting breakfast, my father was home from work, his mother was over with several other women as well as the midwife. I did not have any idea what was going on. When my father looked around and saw me, he said Mother was not feeling too good, and that I was to eat my breakfast and go with one of our neighbors. I was told that I would be back in a few hours. I was gone for about four hours, and when I returned there was a baby. I remember my father picking me up so that I could see the baby and behold there was a tiny baby in bed with Mother. I wanted to touch the baby and my father let me touch him.

As time moved forward, my brother and I grew. My mother seemed to be busy most of the time. As small as I was, I began to notice that she did not play with us as much as she had once done. She did not read us stories or sing little songs to us. When my brother was two years old, I realized that there was something desperately wrong, but I did not know what it was. My father continued to work, he bought his money home, but things did not seem to be going as well as before. Being a child, it did not ring a bell with me. My father was making as much money or more than before, but he was not bringing all of his money home. Each week the money was less than the week before. Mother began to wonder and then to worry about the money, but she did not say anything. Through a neighbor, Mother found out that our father was drinking, gambling, and having an affair. Her heart was broken but by this time she found out that she was pregnant with their third child. What was she going to do? There was less money and food in the house and things began to get worse and soon things got progressively worse. There soon was hardly any food in the house for my brother and me. We began to cry because we were hungry and too small to provide for ourselves. Mother said that she believed our grandmother on our father's side knew what was going on, but was too ashamed to acknowledge it. Evidently he had done this same thing to his first wife and children. She helped Mother as much as she could. Mother did not have any decent clothes. The clothes that she had were so shabby until she was ashamed to come outside of the house. We really needed money to buy the necessary things to survive.

Mother said that our father would come home and he would cry and apologize for what he had done. He would take care of us for a while then he would go back and do the same thing again. He kept doing this over and over. Mother was tired of his behavior. What was she to do? She did not have any money, no job to support herself and her children, and to top that off, she was pregnant. She knew nothing else to do but pray. Mother always prayed, but she began to really pray and ask God for directions. She knew that God heard her, but things had not changed. It got to where my father was not coming home when he got paid on Fridays. One Saturday, my brother and I were crying again because we were hungry. My Mother had a little flour, an egg, and almost a cup of sugar. She took the flour, egg, and a little water and mixed them together and made several pancakes. She took the sugar and made sugar syrup to pour over our pancakes. She did not try to eat anything even though she and the baby needed food. After eating the pancakes there was no more food in the house. My father's mother came to see us that evening, and saw there was no food. She bought enough food to last for a week.

Late Saturday evening, my father came home. He did not say where he had been and my mother did not ask him. Mother had continued to seek God for directions. My father was not worried because my mother could not leave him. There was not any place for her to go. Where would a woman go with two children and a third child on the way? Mother again asked God for His help and what was she to do. God answered her. She said he spoke to her as plain as if He were in the room with her. He told her to go back to her father's home.

On Monday, my father went to work. My mother washed our few clothes including hers and ironed them. She left a couple of shabby outfits out for the week and the other clothes she packed in an old suitcase and pushed it under the bed. She cleaned the house, mopped the floors, changed the linen, washed it and put clean linen on the beds. She was busy all week. She did not see or hear from him on Friday after payday. On Saturday, Father came home again and did not say where he had been. On Monday morning after he left for work Mother bathed us, put clean clothes on us, and we left for the train station. Mother felt that her parents would let her come home and after the baby was born, she planned to get a teaching position in the school district where her parents were living.

My mother went back to her parents' home. Mother's father allowed her to come home, but he told her that if she was going to leave her husband, then leave him. He was not going to allow her to be running back and forth from his house to her husband's house. Mother was not beaten. I do not believe that my father would have ever hit my mother but she was mentally abused by his actions. She believed that he cared for her and that he loved his children, but it seemed as if he could not be faithful as a father and a husband. Mother knew that she could not wait around until he made up his mind as to what he wanted to do. I was too young to remember everything that happened to us when we lived with our father and when Mother left him. My mother told me about the things that happened as I grew older.

As Mother and I talked, I told her that I remembered one thing that happened when they were married. I was four years old and my brother was almost three years old. I remember that he got a drum for Christmas and I got a doll. I remember seeing my father and mother on Christmas morning lying in bed and watching us play with our Christmas toys. I remember that I was swinging my doll by one of her arms and it come a loose from her body. I then sat on my brother's drum and busted it. My mother said, "You remembered that?" and I said "Yes". She said, "Well I do say. That really did happen just as you said." We did not have any other toys to play with that I knew of. I don't know what we ate for Christmas dinner or if we got any fruit or clothes for Christmas or anything else other than the drum and the doll. By the look on my mother's face, I believe she was happy that I could not remember anything else about living with our father.

According to my mother, our father came to visit us often after she left him. He was trying to get her to come back to him. She said he swore he had thought about what he had done and had changed. Mother said she was not taking any chances on what he was saying because we were safe. We had a place to stay and plenty of food to eat. Deep in her heart Mother loved our father and he loved her but she did not believe that he had changed. When he saw that she was not coming back, he did not come very often until my baby brother was born. Only because he wanted to see the baby.

Chapter 9

MOTHER WALKS OUT ON DAD

As soon as she could, my mother filed for a divorce. The lawyer told her she could get child support, but we would have to spend summers with our father. He told one of his family members that when we came to spend the summer with him, he was going to take us and leave. He said no other woman was going to take his children from him. My mother did not file for child support because she did not know what he would do if we went to spend summers with him. My mother did not take us back to see any of our father's people when we were small. We did not know any of our father's people. My grandmother, on my father's side, died when I was six years old so I never knew her. I remember seeing my grandfather on my father's side only once before his death. My father had a sister, a brother, and his brother's children. I met my father's older children by his first wife - my sister, my brother, and later my baby sister who was younger than all of us. I was grown before I first saw all of these family members. My mother never discussed with us why she never took us to see our relatives.

After Mother had given birth to my baby brother and was able to get on her feet again, she applied for a teaching position in the county where she lived with her parents. She was hired, but I don't know where her first teaching assignment was located. When I was six years old, she was assigned to the school which was a church and was across the road from our grandparents' home. As well as I could remember the schools for black students were held in churches. Black children attending school for the first time started in the primer grade. After which they went on to first grade through eighth grade and finally on to high school. When we started high school, no one had to pay for us to continue our education. When Mother started teaching at the church school, she taught primer through eighth grade. There were so many children in the community that Mother was given a teacher to help her. I cannot remember how long she stayed, but my mother did not look so tired at the end of the school day. Mother continued her education after returning home. She went to school during the summer months. Grandmother and my aunt kept us while Mother was in school. She graduated from college in May, 1955, with a Bachelor of Science degree in Elementary Education. Later, she attended graduate school. She would return from school each year as happy as a child with a new toy. I don't think she ever got tired of learning and teaching school.

During her years of teaching, children loved to come to school. There were no buses. Children had to walk. Some children had to walk for miles on dirt roads to get to school. When it rained, the roads were muddy. Mud got on their feet and between their toes. They could not wear their shoes so they would carry their shoes and socks in their hands and when they got to our house, they would hold their feet under the pump, pump water on them to wash the mud away, dry their feet, and put on their nice shoes and socks. We had gravel roads so we did not have to walk on dirt roads. I believe that the only reason we had gravel roads was because there were white people who lived up from us and the roads were for their benefit.

When Mother talked about her teaching career, you could hear the joy in her voice. She had approximately 30 or more kids in a one-room school. They were in various grades from primer through eighth. They were obedient children and she did not have to waste a lot of time trying to keep them quiet and focused on their lessons. Another thing she said about teaching in those days was that you had total parental support. If a child did something that was unacceptable, all the teacher had to do was notify the parents. Parents in those days put the fear of God in their children. Anyone in the neighborhood could reprimand your child and no one was going to say a thing because they knew that it was done in love. No parent would have thought about getting angry with an adult for telling their children what to do and what was right and wrong. It really did take a whole village to raise a child. It would never have entered the minds of children to curse or hit a teacher.

All of the students who attended the school were the children of farmers. Some children had it better than others. Since there was no cafeteria in the one-room schools, parents who could afford it, would give their children a quarter every day to buy their lunch. Their lunches would be bought at the store. My mother would make a list of those students who wanted to buy their lunch and what they wanted. She would send two reliable students to the store with the list and money to buy the lunches. In those days, you could buy three slices of bologna or liver cheese, lunch meat or salami, crackers, and a drink for a quarter. Some kids bought lunch from home in a brown paper bag. I can't ever remember us, my cousins and my mother's children, buying any lunch. I do not know if we bought a lunch from home. I am sure that our cousin Alex either bought his lunch or his parents sent him his lunch because they owned the store where the children were buying their lunches.

After lunch, the children had recess time. The big boys and girls played ball, the small children played a game call "Rise Sally Rise" and the boys and girls could ride on what was then called the "Flying Jenny". It could also be used as a seesaw.

The Flying Jenny was a long two-by-four bolted to a piece of solid wood measuring about three feet long with about one foot of this solid piece of wood driven into the ground. The piece of two-by-four which was bolted to the piece in the ground was stable, but not bolted too tight to keep it from going around and around when the people sitting on each end used their feet to build up a very high speed. When you reached a high speed, you would raise your feet and the Flying Jenny would be going so fast that you had to hold on for dear life to keep from falling off. My grandmother would sometimes sit on the front porch and watch the kids on the playground play the different games. She loved to see the children having fun and enjoying themselves.

As Mother and I sat on my front porch one particular summer and talked about her life, she remembered things about us as children. We laughed and talked about these things, some were happy and some were sad to remember. I remembered a lot of the sad things that happened to my Uncle Jessie's kids, my siblings, and me.

We, like my mother, did not get the opportunity to go to school for nine consecutive months when we were young children. We had to stop and gather the crops then we could go to school. As well as I can remember, we went to school for two months in the summer and five months in the winter. My cousin and I had other duties to do that kept us out of the field. White kids would come by on the bus and they would have the windows down. They would stick their heads out of the windows and yell at blacks in the field. It would be hard to hear what they were saying because the bus would make so much noise while rolling over the gravel on the road. Some people said that the children were using racial slurs. If they were, there wasn't anything that could be done about it. In those days, a black man wasn't valued much more than an animal to some white people.

One Saturday, one of our neighbors took Mother to a town about 18 miles from our home to take care of some business. She took me with her. We were on our way back home and our neighbor had a flat tire. He pulled over to the side of the highway, got out, got the jack and the spare from the trunk of the car. He was changing the tire when a car full of white men came by and they threw a bag full of something on him that smelled like human feces taken from an outdoors toilet. It splashed all over his clothes, his hands, and even got on the side of his face. As they threw this bag, they used racial slurs, and they were falling over laughing. My mother and I were going to get out of the car to see what we could do, but our neighbor told us to get back in the car because they might come back, and if they did, we did not know what they would do. When the flat was fixed, our neighbor brought us home. The smell in the car was so nauseating that it was hard to keep from throwing up in the car. On Monday, we talked about the incident in school and how it affected us, but we had to forget it because there was nothing that could be done about it. Mother did, however, tell the children to tell their parents what happened if they had not already heard. She warned us to be careful when we were out on the highway.

When school was out, my mother got a chance to work in the fields when she was not going to school to keep her teacher's license renewed. When I was nine years old I did not go to the cotton field. My cousin, Grace, and I had to take care of her mother's and our Aunt Ava's babies. Aunt Abbey was Grace's mother.

It was so confining to take care of these babies. We had no time to play and to be little girls. My cousin and I used to say that we never wanted to have children because we had to change the babies' diapers, feed them, rock them to sleep, but sometimes they would not go to sleep. All they did was cry until they tired themselves out and there was not anything else to do but go to sleep. My Aunt Abbey had a son who was a fat baby and he loved to eat. When he got hungry he could make some noise. Sometimes Aunt Abbey and the rest of the family would work a little passed what we called "quitting time". When this happened, Will would start crying because he wanted to eat. It was Grace's duty to take care of him but she would get tired, so Grandmother would make me take him to help her because I was older. I would pinch him to make him holler louder so Aunt Abbey would come home and nurse him. We would be so tired at the end of the day that Grace said we should let the chickens eat the babies. Being so young, she did not have sense enough to know that chickens did not eat babies.

When not taking care of babies, we and those cousins who were not babysitting or not in the field, all got together and had some good times. The times that we got to play, we sometimes got into some "devilment" as the old people would say. I remember that my mother would let me go to my Uncle Jessie's home because he had girls. I was the only girl in our house with four boys. They did not like to play with me so I got to go to my uncle's house to play. For some reason, baby chickens at both my uncle's and at our home began to disappear. My mother, grandmother, and uncle thought that weasels or foxes were eating the baby chickens. Nothing was eating them. We were catching the baby chickens, killing, and burying them so my cousin Lenny (whom we called Little Brother) would preach their funeral. When we got caught, we got a good whipping. We never did that again.

We had so much fun when we were together. We were so close to each other. We were all like sisters and brothers instead of cousins. We, like my mother's sisters and brothers, were not allowed to fight one another. We were poor but we did not know it. There was so much love in our family that the love showed to us overshadowed the knowledge of being poor.

At this time, there were no welfare checks or food stamps. If there were, we did not know anything about them. All of the food that we ate was not bought with welfare checks or food stamps. The food that we ate was grown in the garden, truck patches, hog pens, and hen houses. We got to eat as much as we could hold. No children that we knew ever went to bed hungry. It may not have been the kind of food that we wanted to eat, but whatever the food was, there was plenty of it. What was cooked for you, you ate. There was no such thing as saying "I don't want this!" or "I don't like that!" You ate what was put before you or you did not eat at all. The food that we ate was not fancy types of food, but it was nourishing. We surely did not have a problem of obesity, not in our family or in any of our neighbors' families. On any given day through the week, and for dinner on Saturdays and Sundays, you could walk into the house and smell the scent of either a pot of collard greens, turnips greens, mustard greens, or a pot of either crowder peas, black-eyed peas, or field peas coming from the kitchen.

No matter what kind of food we had during the week, we always had some kind of dessert but we did not have any meat until winter. However, sometimes Sunday was an exception. I don't know how it happened and why it did not happen during the week, but we knew when it was Sunday because we had some kind of meat. We would have smothered steak with gravy and rice or fried chicken with gravy and rice with plenty of good hot biscuits. Sometimes we had squirrel or rabbit with rice and gravy for dinner. I can remember the times when we had baked raccoon or possum with sweet potatoes for Sunday dinner. There was no way that our families were going to let us starve. We would awake to that smell of food on Sunday morning and the smell made us eager to get up.

No matter how eager we were to eat, we all were to wash our face and hands before coming to the table to eat our meals whether it was breakfast or dinner. We had to pour water in the face basin and wash our face and hands. I was raised in the house with four boys and I used to tell on the boys because they would dip the tip of their fingers in the water bucket and wipe their fingers around their eyes and say that they had washed their face and hands. I would tell because I did not want anyone to drink the water after they had put their fingers in it. They would have to go to the pump and pump a fresh bucket of water. Grandmother would tell them if they did it again they were going to get a whipping. In those days all you had to do was tell a child that he or she was going to get a whipping and they would be afraid to do whatever they had done again. Grandmother started watching them when it was time to wash their face and hands, but they did not know that they were being watched. I used to believe adults had eyes in the back of their head because their backs would be turned and they could tell you what you were doing. Grandmother really did not have to watch them again because the mentioning of a whipping ended that problem.

As Mother and I talked about the things we got into as children she could always find a way to bring education into the conversation and the reasons why we needed to stay in school to prepare ourselves for the future. I wanted her to continue telling me about things we did as children. She would laugh and go back to talking about us as children. She would say we were not bad kids; we were just mischievous.

I remembered some of the things we did. One time I remember that we all were down to my Uncle Jessie's house and he had pulled up his crop of peanuts and put them on the top of an old shed. He used a ladder to climb up to put the peanuts on top of this shed. He told us that when they dried, we would get some of them to eat, and the rest would be put up for the winter. We wanted to eat some of the green peanuts, five of Uncle Jessie's children and I climbed up the ladder and got on top of the shed to get the peanuts. Just as we got on top and started eating peanuts, we saw Uncle Jessie coming across the little bridge that separated his house from his brother's house. We did not have time to use the ladder to get down because we would have had to come down one at a time. One of our cousins, Alyssa said, "Let's jump off of the shed." The shed was covered with sheets of tin. A piece of the tin was not nailed down and was sticking up. Our cousin, Elizabeth, slid off of the shed and the tin cut a big gash in her leg. Our uncle was angry, but I cannot remember if he whipped us. He did, however, take Elizabeth to the doctor. The doctor cleaned and stitched the gash on her leg. Over 40 years have passed since that incident and Elizabeth still has that scar on her leg to remind her of what we were doing on top of that shed.

When some of these things happened, our grandfather, Papa was still living; but he had passed a long time before the peanut incident. Uncle Jessie's only children who probably would have remembered Papa was Lenny, Grace, and Eugene. The other children had not been born.

Chapter 10

PAPA DIED

I was seven years old when Papa died. He died on June 2, 1951. I was going to be eight years old in December. I remember that Papa looked like a white man. He used to sit on the porch and he would have us get in a line and we would march passed him and he would tap us with a little switch from a willow tree. The taps that he gave us did not hurt. We would laugh and he would laugh with us.

Papa never wanted to see us get a whipping. Grandmother said if Papa had lived we probably would not have been worth a dime. One day my Aunt Abbey was trying to whip Lenny but he ran under the house and would not come out. She was down on her knees throwing little pieces of wood at him. She was trying to make him come out from underneath the house. Papa came by, saw what she was doing and asked her if she was crazy. He told her that she could hit that boy and hurt him. He found Uncle Jessie at his brother Myles' house and told him that he needed to go home because his wife was trying to kill their son. She was not going to kill him. But evidently whatever he did merited a whipping.

These are things I can remember about Papa - he was a kind man, he spent time with us, and showed us that he loved us and wanted the best for us. The day he died was a sad day for his children and his grandchildren who were old enough to remember him. I remember my mother and my Aunt Clair crying. Not only were his daughters crying but his sons were crying as well. I remember that Aunt Clair was returning home after finishing cosmetology school out west. As she was entering the house she was completely distraught. I believe that her brother, Uncle Jessie was holding her up to keep her from falling. I cannot remember if her baby brother and his family brought her home or if she came home on the train. All I remember is that the adults were crying and we were afraid.

After Papa died things began to change but not drastically at first. We were too young to notice the changes until we were older. We were young and our parents protected us from anything that they felt would hurt us. As far as we were concerned life was good. Underneath the shadows of those good times we had no knowledge of what was going to happen in years to come, but there was a terrible storm brewing.

Chapter 11

CHURCH TOOK OVER

We continued to laugh and play with family members and with neighbor-hood children whenever we got the chance. Sometimes we could visit other children in their homes on a Sunday after Sunday school. We had Sunday school every Sunday if the weather permitted. We would have classes in the back of the church, in the choir stand, in the center of the church, and on each side of the church. We utilized every available space in the church because there were so many young people. We had to go to Sunday school because we had no choice as to whether we wanted to go or not. Our parents did not ask if we felt like going. We had to be almost dead in order to stay home. We looked forward to going because it was the only time that we got a chance to have every young person in the same room other than at school. We could have input concerning the lesson, tell what the lesson meant to us, and how it could shape our lives as young Christians.

We had worship services on the third Sunday of each month. In small communities like ours, we did not have worship services every Sunday because the minister was the pastor of more than one church.

The members were assessed a dollar and some change each worship Sunday. The amount paid did not leave the minister much after church expenses were paid. So, there was no way for him to preach at the same church every Sunday. I cannot remember anyone not paying their church dues, because the church secretary would call the names of each member and they would say out loud the amount that they were assessed. When we were growing up we never heard of anyone "paying tithes".

While the money was being collected for church dues, the members would sit and talk quietly until all dues were collected. Mother as well as other parents did not allow us to talk or laugh out loud while dues were being collected. We could talk quietly and laugh, but it had to be done softly. The amount of dues collected was totaled and the total was announced so that all members could hear the amount for that Sunday.

At no time did women and men or boys and girls sit together in church. The men and boys sat on one side of the church and the women and girls sat on the opposite side. The deacons would have the deacons' period which consisted of scripture, song, and prayer. The choir would sing. Sometimes when we had a pianist, we had beautiful music and when we did not, we sang a cappella. With or without music, we gave our best to God. The adults always encouraged us to do our best for the Lord. The church would be overflowing with people because there were so many families. I remember one third Sunday I was chewing gum in the choir stand. One of the ushers came to me with a fan in his hand. He placed the fan under my chin. He wanted me to take the gum out of my mouth and place it on the fan. I knew what he wanted but instead of taking the gum out of my mouth, I spit on the fan. The children in the choir laughed and I had the nerve to laugh also because I thought I was being funny. I got in big trouble for that incident. I never chewed gum again in church.

We had Baptist Young Peoples Union (BYPU) every Sunday evening just like we had Sunday school every Sunday morning until the weather got bad. It was fun to go to BYPU because there was a lady who made the best ice cream on this side of Heaven. She would sell a cone of ice cream for a nickel. Every child was blessed to have a nickel to buy an ice cream cone. She always sold us the ice cream cones after we were dismissed from our BYPU classes. While eating the ice cream cone we could laugh and talk with each other. Our parents would be there with us because there were classes for them also. Parents and children could visit a while before going home.

The church still had to make plans for its annual revival services in August. Adults and children looked forward to our revival. Revival was held once a year beginning Monday night before the third Sunday. This was the time that those of us who were not saved were given a chance to accept Jesus Christ into our lives. We had to go to what they called the "mourner's bench" and we were to stay there until Christ came into our lives. Now, we had to pray and ask Christ to come in. The first time that I got on the mourner's bench, I did not feel anything and I felt that Christ was not in my life. When the doors of the church were opened, I sat there because I did not "have religion". I did not know that you were not saved by feelings, but by believing that Christ is the Son of God, and that He died for our sins and rose on the third day.

The first time I went to the mourner's bench, I was eleven years old. I had heard some of the older people say that we had to be saved by the time we were twelve years old because after twelve our parents were no longer responsible for our sins. I had heard people in church talk about walking across hell on a spider web and how God had kept them safe. Some of these people were rather fat. I wondered how in the world could these people, as fat as they were, walk across hell on a spider web and not fall in. I went back to the mourner's bench a year later at the age of twelve. We were told to go over to someone whom we believed in, shake hands with this person, and ask them to pray for us. I remember going over to one of the mothers of the church, I shook hands with her and asked her to pray for me.

She could really pray. I remember her asking the Lord to help me believe that Jesus was the Son of God, He came, died for our sins, and He arose on the third day. If we believed that Jesus was the Son of God, that He died for our sins and God raised Him from the dead on the third day, we were saved. I believed and I accepted Christ as my personal Savior.

I was told by my mother about my first birth (natural), but I remember that second birth (spiritual). I will never forget Thursday night, August 9, 1955. This was the night that Christ came into my life and I accepted Him as my personal Savior. When the "doors of the church were opened", I came off of the mourner's bench shouting. The Spirit of God was all over me. As children we used to laugh at the older people when they shouted, but this night was no laughing matter. I was saved and without a doubt I knew it. We did not have a baptismal pool in our church, so we were baptized in a large lake. There would be some spirit filled singing and shouting at the lake. After being baptized, we went back to the church to receive the "right hand of fellowship" from the members of the neighborhood who made up the church and for our regular third Sunday services.

We had Sunday school every Sunday morning and BYPU every Sunday evening, but we only had night services during revival because people had to get up the next morning and work in their fields. During revival time, it was amazing to watch people who had worked all day in the fields, and see how they hurried to get to church during revival. They were almost in a trot to get there. As they neared the church on foot and heard the singing, they would move so fast that we, as children, had to almost run to keep up.

The church would be full of families from the community. We had no air or fans. We had to leave the windows open, fan ourselves with whatever we had to use as a fan, and fight the mosquitoes that came through the windows to feed on us. No one let these things interfere with their praising the Lord while fanning and fighting mosquitoes. As we talked, Mother and I remembered and began to name the number of families in our neighborhood. Most of these families, as well as I could remember, had children. The ones who did not have children were still an integral part of the neighborhood. They had input in what went on in the neighborhood and the church and they could reprimand us as well as any other of the families if we did anything wrong. I often think of these families, and how they loved us. We respected them and they always carried themselves in a manner that made us as children want to carry ourselves in a manner that no one would have anything to say that was unbecoming to us or to our parents. I often remember the neighbors who sat on their front porch on Sunday evenings and watched us as we went to and fro. We would always be on our best behavior because an adult's word was the law. We knew not to go against what adults were saying and our parents were not going to say the neighbors were lying on us. I look at how things have changed since we were children. We did not want anybody to think that we were undisciplined children and that there was no hope for us. The principles that we were raised by and lived by have changed drastically.

They were the only moral principles that we knew. We had great times in our neighborhood while living, growing up, and being taught these principles.

CHAPTER 12

CHRISTMAS TOGETHER

Among those great times were the Christmas holidays. We would be excited months before Christmas. When we were in school we could hardly wait to get outside at recess so that we could talk about what was being cooked for the Christmas holiday and what we were going to get for Christmas. Around Thanksgiving, it was hard to contain our excitement. Even though we were on our best behavior, we were told if we were bad, Santa Claus could see us and know who was good and who was bad. Every child in the neighborhood had a written list or a mental list of the things that we wanted Santa to bring us. We never got everything we wanted, but we loved whatever we got. We were young and we did not know that our parents had to pay for the things we got for Christmas. We were told that Santa Claus was at the North Pole making toys for every child in the world. On Christmas Eve, his elves were packing his sleigh so he could make his trip around the world to deliver toys to kids.

I don't recall that we ever went to a store or anywhere else to see Santa Claus to tell him what we wanted. We saw pictures of Santa Claus in books. All of the Santa Clauses were big white men with long white hair, a long white beard, and dressed in a red suit with a red hat trimmed in white, along with black boots with white at the top. We were afraid of the pictures of Santa Claus when we were very small. For the life of me, I don't know why. Mother told us that we did not have to be afraid of Santa Claus because he loved children and he was a kind man.

While in school, waiting until the time to get out for the holiday, we would sometimes stray away from our studies and be in a world of our own daydreaming about Christmas until Mother, who was the teacher, would remind us to stay on task.

The baking of cakes and pies would be going on in every house in the neighborhood while we were in school, as well as after we got home from school. Children would talk about the kinds of cakes and pies that were being made to eat throughout the holidays. It was exciting because cakes and pies were not common everyday food to us like they are to the children of today. We would have some kind of dessert at dinner time every day of the week, but the dessert would be some type of cobbler, and was unlike the pies in a shell for Christmas. We very seldom had a cake unless it was a sheet cake without icing.

In our house, Aunt Clare would be the one doing the baking. When we would get home from school we could lick the spoon and scrape the bowl to get what little cake batter was left. When we would walk into the house from school the whole house would smell like Christmas because cakes were baking in the oven. There was one cake that was made once a year, only at Christmas, that was a coconut cake. Everyone loved it, so we had about three of them every Christmas. We had chocolate cakes, lemon cakes, pound cakes, jelly cakes, caramel cakes, and tea cakes. The tea cakes we could eat, but not any of the other cakes until Christmas. We had a lot of cakes, but we never had 40 cakes as Grandmother did when Mother and her siblings were children. There was no cake mix that I knew of. Aunt Clare would make all of these cakes from scratch including the icing, and these cakes would be beautifully decorated with nuts and colorful candy. It was a joy just to look at them.

When it was time to make the pies, the crusts for the pies were not store bought. They were homemade. We had sweet potato pies, lemon pies, egg custard pies, and apple pies. We did not have a lot of different kinds of pies, but we had a great number of the ones that Aunt Clare made. We could give some away and still have a lot left. We could look at all of the good desserts but we could not touch a one of them.

Butchering time was done in December so that we would have fresh meat and have our pork shoulder for Christmas breakfast and dinner. We would also have either a turkey, goose, or several ducks plus dressing, plenty of vegetables, candied sweet potatoes, potato salad, homemade rolls, cornbread, and plenty of other goodies. Christmas dinner was the best dinner of the year because there was so much food. During the holidays, we could eat until we were so full that our stomachs would not hold another bite. We were taught to ask for what we wanted on our plates instead of just getting it. When we asked for extra food on our plates we had to eat it. We did not throw any food away. If "your eyes were bigger than your stomach" as my grandmother would say, you still had to eat everything on your plate. If you were just being greedy putting more food on your plate than you were going to eat and you had to eat it, you would think twice before doing this again.

Leading up to the holiday, Mother would come home from school when she could and help Grandmother and Aunt Clare with the cooking. Mother could not leave school at 3:30 p.m., because she did not have a janitor to clean the floor so she had to sweep the floor herself. Sometimes children who lived close to the school would stay behind and sweep for her and erase the blackboards. We would also stay when no one else could and sweep the floor. Mother did a lot of her paper work at school so that she did not have to bring it home with her. When she did this, it gave her more time to help her mother and her sister.

The closer it got to the Christmas holiday, the more excited we became. We would come home from school to the smell of apples. We would say that we smelled apples and Grandmother would say that we smelled apples because that was what we wanted. We believed what she was saying that there were no apples in the house. We often wondered down through the years if there were no apples in the house, then why did we smell apples around Christmas time and at no other time during the year? When we were growing up, we did not get fruit like children do today. An apple was a treat because we only got big red apples once a year and that was at Christmas. The apples were really in the house, but grandmother, Mother, and Aunt Clare did not want us to know that we actually did smell apples. It would take away the excitement of getting them on Christmas morning.

It is amazing how apples could be smelled throughout the house then and the apples you buy today leave no scent in the house or in the stores where there are large numbers of apples. When we were told that there were no apples in the house, we did not keep asking questions. We accepted what we had been told, but it did not stop us from wondering what was in the house that smelled like apples. When we were older, we laughed about those days. The apples were in the house and were hidden in a small attic above the pantry in the kitchen. They stayed there until they were put in our shoe boxes on Christmas Eve along with nuts, raisins, an orange, and candy.

It seemed as if Christmas would never come. To us as children, it seemed as if time stood still. Instead of a day having 24 hours, it seemed more like a day had 48 hours. Of course, time was not standing still. It only seemed like that to us as children. I think that children can wish for Christmas to come so badly that they cannot think of anything else other than Santa Claus is coming and he is going to give us toys. According to us, we had been good children so we could not think of any reason he would not give us our toys.

We would try to do everything right and do everything that Grandmother, Mother and Aunt Clare told us to do. Grandmother would tell us that we had better watch ourselves so that we would not do anything bad. We would try to remember if we had done something bad. It was hard to be really good for a whole year. Sometimes we would torment ourselves, by trying to justify some of the things that we had done. But we did not think that they were as bad as what some other children had done. The main thing was to please Santa Claus so that we would get our toys.

Finally, the day before Christmas arrived; it was finally Christmas Eve. The house smelled so good and it was very clean. The meat was baking in the wood burning oven and a delicious aroma was coming from the kitchen that went throughout the whole house. When we were small, I could never understand why my mother would take my two cousins (whom my grandmother was raising and who lived in the house) and my two brothers and I to Uncle Jessie's house on Christmas Eve to get their hair cut. Uncle Jessie cut hair and there would be a lot of little excited girls and boys. Their fathers sat all over the place waiting to get their hair cut and their sons' hair cut so that the children could go home, get in the bed, and go to sleep so Santa Claus could come. There was no father in our house to take my cousins and brothers to get their hair cut so my mother took them, and I had to go with them. What we did not know then was the haircuts were done on Christmas Eve because they were trying to keep us up as late as possible so that we would fall asleep as soon as we laid our heads on the pillow. Then they would be able to put our toys out and would not have to worry about us waking up before morning.

Christmas Eve was so beautiful then. We lived out in the country where there were not any street lights. It would be dark, but the moon would give such a radiant light that it almost looked like daylight. The moon beams looked like clear prisms and they casted their light for miles over the fields and all of the homes. You could see lights through the windows of some of the neighbors' homes and know that they were feeling the same love, laughter, warmth, and happiness we were feeling in our home. I don't ever recall seeing a cloudy Christmas Eve night. There may have been some, but I cannot remember them. This night was different from any other night of the year. Everything was serene and quiet. There were no sounds of dogs barking or any other sounds. The night was hallowed. It was the night of the birth of Jesus Christ. It seemed at any time the heavens would open and the sky would be full of angels singing and praising the Lord.

Even though it was cold, there was a warmth that came from the moon beams that seemed to warm the entire world. We always walked to Uncle Jessie's house. This gave us the chance to have our own thoughts about Christmas, but we did not have to share these thoughts unless we wanted. Before leaving home, the radio announcer would be saying that Santa Claus would soon be on his way to deliver toys to all of the children in the world. We would have heard songs like *"Silver Bells"*, *"Silent Night"*, *"Santa Claus is Coming to Town"*, *"Merry Christmas"*, *"Oh*

Little Town of Bethlehem", "White Christmas", and many other songs. These songs would resound in our heads. I always liked *"Silver Bells"* because in the large cities I could visualize the beautifully decorated city sidewalks, stores, and the thousands of people busily shopping, carrying arms full of Christmas gifts wrapped in beautiful colored paper, and people happily exchanging Christmas greetings. Children filled with joy would be looking in store windows telling their parents to take them in the store, not only to see the toys but also wanting their parents to buy them every toy in the store. To us, Christmas Eve was a holy night.

Before we left on Christmas Eve going to Uncle Jessie's house for the boy's haircuts, there was a lady who played Santa Claus. She would come to every house where there were children. Grandmother and Mother would tell us that Santa Claus was going back to the North Pole after he had checked to see who had been naughty or nice. Mother would tell Santa Claus that we had been pretty good and he could stop by our house when he started delivering toys.

We did not know that this was one of our neighbors who was wearing a Santa mask, had long white hair, a white beard, a red and white Santa suit, gloves and black boots. Also at the time, we did not know that this was a woman playing Santa Claus. She was very large. In later years, we learned who she was and even though she was large, she stuffed her suit with pillows to make herself even larger. Her visits brought joy to so many children.

Santa Claus was not the only visitor that we had on Christmas Eve. There was another woman who visited everyone on Christmas Eve whether they had children or not. She made fruit cakes in small foil pans. Early on Christmas Eve, her husband would drive her around to every house in the neighborhood to deliver fruit cakes. I think that everyone looked forward to this because she made the best fruit cakes. Every year when she bought the fruit cakes, my mother and Aunt Clare would cut the cake and have a glass of elderberry wine that they had made. We would get to eat a small piece of the cake, but we did not get any wine. Why we did not get any wine, I do not know because it tasted like grape juice. We slipped one time and drank some and it did not do a thing to us or for us.

On Christmas morning, we would wake up, jump out of our beds overly excited, and look down beside our beds in a shoe box and we would see our Christmas toys. In each of our boxes, we would find an apple, orange, raisins on a stem, nuts, candy, and our toys. I got a doll, a set of little dishes, and doll clothes. My brothers and cousins got silver cap guns with a holster. The paper caps made a loud sound when they put them in the gun and pulled the trigger. We also got firecrackers. We could go outside, light the firecrackers, and listen to the loud sounds they made. You could hear the sound of firecrackers all over the neighborhood. We never celebrated the Fourth of July so we never had firecrackers until Christmas. After being outside for a while shooting firecrackers, we would come in, make our beds, take a sponge bath, put on our clothes, and play with our toys again until it was time to eat breakfast.

Christmas was always so much fun in our house as well as in our uncles' homes with their families. I remember one Christmas my cousin Chuck got up, saw his toys, and was so excited. He had on what we called then a one-piece undergarment known as "unions". I guess they would be called thermal underwear now. The unions had an opening in the front and an opening in the back. The back part of the undergarments had a square piece that could be unbuttoned when one had to use the bathroom. Chuck began to jump and yell. Grandmother thought Chuck was jumping and yelling because he was becoming overly excited about his toys. She said that this boy is going to be sick if he does not settle down. What she did not know was a piece of red hot coal had jumped out of the wood heater onto the floor and Chuck had stepped on it. He was not jumping because he was excited, he was jumping because he had stepped on that piece of coal, and it had burned the bottom of his foot. When he got through jumping, the whole square flap in back of his unions had become unfastened and his whole behind was showing. When grandmother saw that she said, "Lord, help us!"

As we grew older, each Christmas became better and better. Christmas was truly even more exciting when we started having Christmas lights and Christmas trees. Mother, Grandmother, and Aunt Clare still used the shoe boxes that our winter shoes came in for our toys. The boxes were placed by our beds instead of under the

Christmas tree. We decorated the tree and ate lots of hot dogs before going to Uncle Jessie's house again for the Christmas Eve hair cuttings. Each Christmas we celebrated breakfast using the slave master's last name. The breakfast was known as the Breakfast Tradition, the same tradition used by the slave master, our great, great grandparents, great grandparents, grandparents, and parents. We, the grandchildren, ate the same thing they ate. We had cold pork shoulder, sardines, hogshead souse, cheese, crackers, and cake. I do not think any of us, our grandfather's grandchildren, have carried on the **breakfast tradition** or have passed it on to our children. I talked to my mother's baby brother before his death, and he told me how he still carried on this **breakfast tradition** at Christmas time. He did not say that he included his family. I thought to myself we have allowed some of our history to die. We are parents, great grandparents, great, great grandparents, and grandparents and we have not taught our children about a tradition that began back in the 1820's. Whether our children follows this tradition or not, we need to tell them about it. It should be carried on by us and generations to come. We should never let it die.

Chapter 13

HEAVEN AND HELL PARTIES

After Christmas was over, things became rather dull especially on Friday nights. We attended school during the week, but it seemed as if something was missing. The weekends were very dull because there was no school over the weekends and we had nothing to do after all of our chores were done. We knew that we would have Sunday school and BYPU, but we wanted something else to do. We were too young to do or plan anything for ourselves.

Since we were too young to go anywhere, plan activities, or do anything on our own outside of our neighborhood for social activities, the neighbors planned activities for us. Mother and I talked about the Heaven and Hell parties that were planned for our enjoyment. These parties were held at the church mainly on Friday nights. Some of the neighbors would use a few of their nice white sheets and divide the church in half. One side of the church represented Heaven, and the other half represented Hell. You had a choice to choose either Heaven or Hell. Whatever side you chose, you had to stay there. You could not leave.

Some of us were afraid to choose Hell because we had heard so many horrible things about it, so we would choose Heaven. If you chose Heaven, you ate ice cream, cake, and drank punch. If you chose Hell, you ate spaghetti filled with hot sauce, bread with hot sauce, and had nothing to drink. If you chose Hell, the people there could hear the people in Heaven laughing, talking, and having a good time. If you chose Heaven, the people there could hear the people in Hell coughing, mourning, gasping for air, and hollering because that hot sauce was tearing them up! We would leave the church laughing, talking, and looking forward to whatever the neighbors were going to plan for us. We did not have an activity every Friday. Sometimes the activities were twice a month, but whenever they were we had a wonderful time.

During the summer months when the hoeing of the cotton was finished and school had started, the neighbors still wanted to have some type of activities for the children at school on Friday nights. The people in the neighborhood and sometimes even the grandparents enjoyed getting out of the house to attend the activities at least twice a month.

Mother was the teacher at Woodson Elementary School and had been for a long time. She was instrumental in getting a white man to come twice a month on Friday nights to show us a movie. He had a movie projector and a large screen that looked like a big piece of cloth. The only movies he had were old black and white westerns. The movie cost ten cents and a bag of popcorn cost ten cents, too. The neighbors would come and bring their kids. We would eat popcorn, watch the movie, and laugh at the funny scenes. We would be so uplifted when it was time to go home. We were kids who did not really have a care in the world. Our world was carefree and we were bursting with joy all in this little one-room classroom.

Chapter 14

THE FOUNDATION I FOUND IN A ONE-ROOM SCHOOL

As I sit here in retrospect and reflect on my education over the years of attending school in a one-room school building and all of the joyful times we spent there, I think about the effect it had on my life as well as the lives of the other children in my class. We may not have known it then but as we grew older and left this one-room school building, we began to realize that the foundation for our continuing education began in this one-room school.

As I reflected on my realization of the foundation of my education that I received in a one-room school, I compared this foundation to that of the Sears Tower Building in Chicago, Illinois and of the Empire State Building in New York. When you look at these sky scrapers you have to know that as they continued to add onto these extraordinary tall buildings, they had to be built on a deep, strong, and solid foundation; otherwise they would not have been able to withstand more weight added to the foundation nor would they have been able to weather the winds, storms, and wear and tear over the years.

This is how I have viewed the foundation for my continuing education beyond the one-room school. The teachers who taught me as well as other students, made sure that we received a deep, strong, and solid foundation in the subject matters that they taught us. They taught us until we were thoroughly able to comprehend the subject matters. Because of this foundation we were able to forge ahead, finish high school, go to some of the best U.S. universities, and compete with students who had no knowledge of a one-room school let alone see one. We graduated with degrees in education, doctoral degrees, and degrees in the medical field. All of these degrees were beyond the bachelor's degree. Our teachers knew the value of an education. They empowered us with the knowledge that we could learn, to know that we had the right to learn, and to never underestimate our ability to strive for the best education available to us.

I am now a senior citizen and I have been gone from that one-room school for over 60 years. I have received several degrees beyond my Bachelor of Science degree, retired from a very rewarding career in teaching, but I still have vivid memories of those years in Woodson Elementary School, a one-room school. They were happy years and the memories will remain with me all of the days of my life.

Over the years, I have had to chuckle to myself as I thought about my education and the foundation it was built on. When I think of this, it always brings to mind the memory of my mother. When I was younger, I thought my mother was an education fanatic. We could be talking about buying material to make a suit or a dress and somehow she would always find a way to bring something into the conversation pertaining to education. In later years, I remember one day in particular. She and I had decided to take a walk around the apartment complex where my husband and I lived. As we began our walk, she asked me if I knew how important an education was, especially to blacks. I thought to myself "Here she goes again!", but amazingly the conversation took a different direction than I had expected.

As we walked, she noticed the beautiful flowers in the flower beds around my neighbors' apartments, and wanted to know why I did not have a single flower bed with flowers in it around my apartment. I asked her, "Do you remember my views about digging in God's earth?" She laughed and said, "I cannot remember what you said about digging in God's earth." I told her that I would refresh her memory. I asked, "Mother, do you remember when I used to chop cotton in the cotton field from sunup to sundown, and I said that when I got grown, finished high school and college, I was going to shake the mud from the Delta off my feet and I would never dig in God's green earth again?" My mother laughed and said, "You do not have any plants around your apartment, so I guess you have been true to your word."

Yes, I have been true to my word. My husband loves to plant flowers and plant a garden. I stand afar and watch him make flower beds when he has time and chop in his garden to remove grass and weeds from around his vegetable plants. I salute him for his endeavors, but I have no desire to help him. Approximately 50 years have passed and I have never dug in God's earth again.

Mother and I continued our walk. We both were quiet as we looked at the beautiful color in the flowers which were not painted with a brush, but by the hand of God. We continued to observe many of the other marvelous handiworks of God. Mother and I were heading to the park not far from my apartment to watch my husband empire a baseball game. We had been quiet for at least 20 minutes or more before Mother spoke again. She wanted to know if she had ever told me about the history of the school district that she was working for and the one black high school in this district that she had not known about until she had been in the school district for several years. I told her that she had not mentioned anything to me about a black high school. Her words to me were, "Remind me to tell you about the history of the district and the one high school for blacks who lived in the northern part of the county." Mother never got around to mentioning the history of the school district again. I do believe that it was her intent to do so, but she passed away years later without ever getting around to continuing that part of our conversation.

I was left in limbo concerning the history of that school district. I allowed many years to pass even though I often wondered what she was going to tell me about the district and where she got information that there was a black high school in the northern part of the school district. No one had mentioned this to us when we were in the one-room school.

We had always heard that there was no high school for blacks in this county. I began to ponder this situation and decided to see if I could find out what my mother was going to tell me about this high school for black students.

It took many years to find out about the black high school in the northern part of the county. With the help of a friend who shared information about this school, I think this was what my mother was going to tell me but never got around to it.

There *was* a high school in the northern part of the county for black students. It was built in 1931 by the Baptist Association. Since it was built by them it was named a Baptist high school after that county. When this school was built my mother was still living with her parents. She was only 20 years old and had finished the eighth grade in 1929 (at the age of eighteen). She was waiting to go to high school as soon as her parents were able to get the money to pay for her to continue her education.

The high school for blacks in this northern part of the county burned in 1947. If anyone knew why it burned it was not mentioned. The students in the northern part of the County Public Schools had no place to continue their education beyond the eighth grade unless their parents were able to pay for them to attend school in other neighboring counties. You may think that their opportunity to continue their education was over, but it was not. Did they give up on continuing their education? No, they did not. They waited and hoped that another school would be built for them. Six years after the burning of the high school, a vocational school was built for black students. The students got to this school by carpooling because there were no buses.

This high school held its first graduation in 1955. I was fortunate enough to know two ladies that graduated with that class. They did not give up hope and they persevered until another school was built for black students.

These students, like all of us in our county during the early years, got our foundation for continuing education in a one-room school building. It was not easy for any of us; therefore, I believe that we owe ourselves a standing ovation because we did not allow dire circumstances to defeat us. I now believe that I have gotten the information about the northern part of the county's school district and the high school for black students that my mother wanted me to know. The third high school built in the county still stands today in all of its magnificence and elegance. It continues to afford the students the opportunity to learn a trade and excel in all of their subject areas. The students have excellent and dedicated teachers certified in their subject areas and have the most modern and state of the art equipment to enhance their opportunities for learning. This school district has come a long way from those one-room school buildings, but for us (the older citizens of this county), we can rejoice because we got our foundation for continuing education whether it was just graduating from high school or going on to the colleges of our choice. The foundation started in those one-room school buildings. This was all that we had, but we wisely used our time for learning and we are grateful for the one-room schools and the teachers who taught us to appreciate the opportunity to learn.

Beyond the walls of those one-room schools and our continuing education, things were still confronting black people.

Chapter 15

EDUCATED OR NOT; WE WERE STILL BLACK

In 1954, when blacks were trying to get registered to vote in the southern states, some whites made it impossible for them to vote by giving them a test that neither educated nor uneducated blacks could pass. On the other hand, white people passed the test whether they were educated or uneducated. There were blacks who did not try to register for fear of losing their jobs. So rather than lose their jobs, they refrained from trying to register to vote. People who staged sit-ins were beaten and put in jail. Even young people who participated were kicked out of school. We used to hear Grandmother, Mother, and Aunt Clare talking, but none of them or the neighbors would try to register to vote. My mother worked for the school district in her county and if she had tried to register to vote, I know she would have lost her job faster than one could blink an eye.

Things grew progressively worse. People in the community did not venture out at night very much. If they had to, someone would always accompany them. There was always news about black people being beaten or killed. Blacks and some whites who were not from southern states, but who came as volunteers to help other black people register to vote, staged sit-ins, and participate in marches to bring nationwide attention to the plight of blacks being denied the right to vote. However, the consequences for trying to help ended up getting some of them killed, sadly enough to say. One incident involved three volunteers (two white men and one black man) who were returning from a southern town known as Philadelphia. They were stopped, killed, and buried in a dam on a farm. The black man had been badly beaten. Things were going to get worse and our families kept us close to home. We were in the house by dusk. I prayed that no one in our house would have the need to go outside to use the outdoor toilet. We had no running water and no inside bathrooms. We did not know what was hiding out in the dark. We did have a chamber pot we called a "slop jar". It was used only to urinate in. If there was anything beyond that, then you went to the outdoor toilet – regardless of rain, shine, sleet, or snow.

Everyone's nerves were on edge and they were wondering what will happen next? One of the most gruesome things happened that anyone had ever heard of. In August 1955, a young black boy from the north was visiting family members in a southern town. He knew that there were some prejudices and segregation in other northern cities, but he knew nothing about the terrible hatred and prejudices in southern states. This was beyond his knowledge. One day he went into a store to purchase candy. On his way out of the store, it was reported that he said, "Bye baby," or something to that effect to the white store owner's wife when he was leaving.

A few nights later two white men went to his uncle's house in the middle of the night and took the boy away. A few days later they found his body in the Tallahatchie River. Some of the gruesome things done to him included: his eyes being gouged out, his skull totally crushed from blunt force trauma, a bullet to the head, and he was also believed to have been castrated. Everyone wondered what did this 14-year old child endure before they killed him? It was the most inhumane and horrific thing anyone had ever heard. His young body was almost unrecognizable. The news reported said that he was identified by a ring he had on his finger.

His mother had his body shipped back to his northern hometown. When his body arrived, she checked to make sure that this body was her son. She insisted that he have an open casket funeral. Thousands upon thousands of people from all over the nation were able to view the body. She wanted the world to see what was done to her son in one of the most prejudiced states in the south. I was 12 1/2 years old when this child died. I saw the pictures in various magazines and so did other people in the community and throughout the nation. We, as children, and the neighbors in our community, had never seen anything that gruesome in our lives. We could not put into words what this child's body and face looked like.

We were held even tighter by our parents and told we were never to cause any trouble with any white person. We had to be on our best behavior even if the white person was wrong. When we went to town we were very respectful when we went into any white owned store. If they did not speak to us, we were to use the money that we made by picking cotton to buy what we went into the store for and leave.

When we were caught up with picking our own cotton, we used to pick cotton for someone else at three dollars per hundred pounds. I could never pick 200 pounds of cotton, but I could pick 150 pounds. I had cousins who could pick 200 pounds and some neighbors who could easily pick 300 pounds. That meant that the cousins were going to get six dollars, and the neighbors were going to get nine dollars. I was satisfied with my four dollars and fifty cents. We had money to go to town and buy something.

We would go home, get washed up, put on clean clothes, and go to town. Many of the neighbors also went so we travelled together. I don't know if this was done for protection, but we were sometimes in groups. After we left town the roads were pitch black because there were no street lights. Being in town and seeing all the lights and all of the people sitting on the street was exhilarating. Some would be laughing and talking and others would be seated on benches outside the stores eating and watching the people go by. We were not allowed to eat on the streets. If we wanted to buy something to eat, we had to buy it and go get in the truck and eat it. I remember one Saturday night I kept going in this man's store and I would buy what we called an Eskimo Pie. It was ice cream on a stick covered with chocolate. I loved those things. I would go in the store and buy one and go to the truck to eat it. I did this eight times. The store owner was listening to the ball game on the radio, and each time I went in there he had to get the Eskimo Pie and get my money. On the eighth time, he got angry and said to me, "Why don't you buy the whole box?" I wanted more of them, but I was afraid to go back in the store. Those Eskimo Pies made me so sick that night. I have not eaten another one to this day. While in town, the blacks sitting around eating and talking seemed to feel safe in a large group.

My mother laughed the day that we were sitting on my porch talking about going to town. My mother always talked to me more about an education than she did my brothers. She said that if I married a man who would not take care of me and our children, if we had any, I could get out on my own and take care of myself and my children. She was adamant about my getting an education. I told her when I was young and we would go to town, I had only one dream. I told her I had said when I was grown, I was going to buy me some lunch meat wrapped in white paper, some crackers, and a drink. I was going to come out of the store, sit on the street, eat my lunch meat, crackers, drink my *Coca Cola*® and watch the people go by. After I had eaten my lunch meat, crackers, and had drunk my drink, I was going back in the store to buy me a pint of ice cream. I was going to eat my ice cream using my own spoon from home and continue to sit and watch people walk up and down the one street in the small town.

I had never been out of a southern state, and I had no idea what was beyond the south. Therefore, I had no place that I could compare to my hometown. I thought that there was nothing better than going to town, sitting on the street, eating, and looking. Little did I know that within a few years I was going to leave my southern state and I was going to find out later that there were prejudices and hatred, but not as visible as in my state and other states in the south.

In May, 1956, my mother's sister Hannah died. All of Mothers' sisters and brothers were at her sister's funeral. After the funeral, I went home with Mother's baby brother, his wife, and their children. I got to see things that I had never seen before. I saw the Painted Desert, Hoover Dam, and we went to some famous outlaw's grave in Arizona.

I can't remember what else I saw. My uncle was in the Army and they lived on the Presidio. I was fascinated by standing on their balcony and looking out over the Pacific Ocean. I did not know that there were so many things to see because I had never travelled outside of the south.

I was fine until it was time to go to school. I did not know that I was going to be in school with white people. I was scared to death. On my first day in school, I met a well-known singer's sister. She was kind to me. We were in the lunch line and I was a nickel short of having enough money to pay for my lunch. I became so frightened because I did not know what the woman on the cash register was going to do to me. The singer's sister gave me the nickel to finish paying for my lunch. From that day forward she befriended me along with a Hispanic girl whose name I have forgotten over the years.

The fear of white people impaired my ability to learn. My typing teacher was so kind to me. I do believe that she knew what I was feeling because she knew I was from the south and I had never known anything but total segregation. Every day when I left my uncle and aunt's home for school, I believed that I would never see them again. All I had known was that white people could kill you and there was nothing you could do about it.

I did not know how to tell my uncle and aunt about what was going on in my life. I suffered from this fear. There were days that my head ached, I was nauseated, and I felt faint because of fear. Classes would be going on, the teachers would be teaching, assignments and tests were given but I did not do them because I would be sitting in class wondering if this was the day that I was going to die or which one of these children were going to kill me. I knew the things that the teachers were talking about but I was afraid to open my mouth. I had not had any trouble learning at home. It got so bad that they thought I had a learning disability. I was put into special education classes. I did not know anything about these classes. We did not have any special education classes in the schools back at home. There may have been some students who were special needs students, but they were put in the classes with regular students and no one paid any attention because no one knew that there was anything wrong with them. We did not have special education teachers or anyone who could detect special needs children.

Chapter 16

MY RETURN TO MISSISSIPPI

I stayed in the west until the summer of 1958. My aunt's mother got very sick so she drove over 900 miles to our home in the south with a 14½ year old teenager (which was me) and three small children (one was a small baby). My aunt had a flat tire in the Arizona desert. She could fix a flat tire but when she checked the jack there were some rivets missing on it. So, there we sat in the middle of the Arizona desert miles from any town. I tried to flag down several cars passing by, but they would not stop. Finally, a car stopped and it was two priests who helped us. They used their jack to raise the car, remove the tire, and took it 50 miles away to have it fixed. They brought it back, put it on the car, and we were on our way. My aunt's baby was so small and it was so hot on her. All of her clothes had been removed with the exception of her diaper. She was hot and she was crying to prove it. My Uncle was stationed in another state and my aunt did not wait for him to get a leave of absence so he could drive her to her mother's funeral. She drove herself and my uncle met her there.

After the funeral, my uncle and aunt along with their three children, made preparations to return to their home on the Presidio Army Base. I did not return with them because my mother missed me terribly while I was away and she wanted to keep me there with her. It was a blessing that she did because I would have still been afraid of white people and what they could do. I hated the area's junior high school with a passion. Not because anyone had mistreated me, but because I was afraid of going where I could easily be killed by a white person. I did not know why I was in this classroom. I had noticed that the children in the special education classes were different than me and the other children who were in the regular classrooms. I became very withdrawn. One day, I was in music class and the music teacher had a sheet of music and the song had the words "nigger" in it. She asked me if I wanted to sing this song and I said "No!" When she went back to her desk to put the music away, a white girl got out of her seat, came over to me and said unkind things to me. I don't believe that the teacher heard her, but I was terrified. I cried that whole class period. I think that day was the most difficult day in my life. I knew that my life was all over. If this girl could say unkind things to me then I knew that there was nothing to keep her from killing me. White people had killed this young black boy from the north and had gotten away with it, hadn't they? They had killed the three Freedom Riders and gotten away with murdering them. What was going to keep this girl from killing me? If I told my uncle and aunt, what was going to keep them from being killed? I lived with my thoughts and fears shut up on the inside of me. I lived daily with the torment of fear. I often wondered what would have happened to me if I had gone back. After finishing high school, there would have been nothing for me to do but possibly become a maid or some other kind of laborer which led to nowhere. I believe with all my heart if I could have shared with my uncle and aunt my fears and what was happening, they would have seen me through this difficult period of my life and I would never have ended up in special education classes. White people at my junior high school were not killing black people, but since I had lived with the killing of blacks, I felt that because they were white it meant that they were capable of killing blacks and could do it at any time and get away with it. I did not see the National Guard in and around the school to protect the black children. Blacks were able to go in the school without being hurt. All of their schools were safe and totally integrated, but I had known only segregation and fear for so many years that it was hard for me to believe that white people would not hurt or kill black people.

When I went out west, I was going to enter the seventh grade at the beginning of school. When I left junior high school, I was in the high eighth grade. At the second semester of that same year, I would have entered the low ninth grade and would have gone to another high school. There I would have finished some of the low ninth grade and completed some of the high ninth grade but I came home. After returning home, my mother enrolled me in a junior high school in the area. Before returning home, I had finished the first half of the eighth grade and was well into the second half. The students there were just beginning the first half of the eighth grade; therefore, I was a whole semester ahead of the students there. After Mother had some kind of discussion with the principal, I started high school as a ninth grader. The day that I entered that school, a place that I had never been before, I felt so comfortable and had no fear of being hurt. Everyone was black like me so I had no reason to be afraid anymore. I did not have to face the fear of being killed by some white person when I got on the bus to go to school and when I entered the school. I felt safe and I did not have to worry. I shared my fears with my mother and she told me there was nothing wrong with it and it was all right to be afraid and I had nothing to be ashamed of.

I was 14½ years old when I returned home and my home state still had a reputation for using scare tactics to frighten black people and to kill someone black was like no harm done. Things had not changed after I returned. If anything, they had become progressively worse. Although we were now teenagers, our parents still kept a close watch over us. They feared for our safety because a lot of the things that happened to blacks were done at night. Teenagers went out in groups when they did go to a movie or other places where teenagers hung out. Our parents were constantly cautioning us to be careful when we were not around them.

During all of the terrible things that were happening in the south, my mother was still teaching school but sometime during the late 1950's she no longer taught in a church. The school district had closed all of their schools that had been held in churches. Black children went to school in churches prior to attending a segregated school which was a part of the northern area of the school district because there were no school buildings in the southern part of the county for black students. This particular school had been a school for whites only. In the southern area of the county where we lived there were a lot of children. When the church schools were closed in our area, many of the students in the upper grades were going to school in another county. The children living in our area of the southern county who were still in elementary school were supposed to attend school in that county but they did not get a chance.

One morning, it was quite a surprise to the black students who boarded the school bus on their way to the junior high school located in another county. When they got there they were not allowed to get off of the bus. They were going to be taken to the school located in the northern part of the school district. There were 14 of us who remained in the southern county school district. Some were ninth graders, some were sophomores, others were juniors, and some were seniors in high school. Those students that were moved were mostly in elementary school and a few were going to be in junior high school at the school in the northern county. A new high school had been built for the white students. A high school was also built for the black students. It was named after a local black school administrator in our district. I don't know what happened to her after the church schools were closed.

The racial issues were still going on. From time to time, I would ask my mother if this was ever going to end. She would always say "In God's time this too will end." My mother and my grandmother always had some encouraging words to pass on to us. My mother would always tell us regardless of what was going on we should focus on our schooling because no one could take from us what we had learned. My grandmother would echo the same. I felt that these were the voices of wisdom speaking to us. I was still young and I did not keep up with all of the racial issues going on in the southern states. A lot of what we knew we learned from our parents and other adults. I think I became more conscious of the racial issues during the early sixties because I read more about it and listened to the news.

My state had been labeled as the most impoverished state in the nation. It was stated that blacks were the ones listed in the highest number of impoverished people. It would really break your heart to see some black people who lived on white plantations and had worked hard and did not have anything to show for the hard work. Their clothes were dirty, raggedy, and of the poorest quality of material. Some were nearly barefooted because the shoes they had on their feet were referred to as "slides" where there was a place to slide your foot in, a sole underneath the foot, but the back of the shoe was open. Some of the children looked malnourished and for others, it looked like their hair had not been combed for weeks. It would have taken someone without a soul not to feel sympathy for these people whom I am sure wanted to do better but could not. Since we did not know these people personally, it was hard to know how they fared during the winter months for clothes and food.

Black people were powerless and needed something to happen that would help them have a voice about what was happening to them. Blacks believed that the right to vote would help. To lend aid to the cause, the Freedom Riders descended upon the southern states for the purpose of trying to get black people registered to vote. They were also helping to end segregation, to help blacks be able to eat at places where it said "whites only" and to use public facilities such as the bathrooms and water fountains. Some blacks did not want to take the risk of being thrown in jail, badly beaten, or bitten by dogs, so they did not dare join in the demonstrations or sit-ins.

There was always something to read or hear about one of the Southern States, Mississippi, which had a bad reputation for committing violations that hindered blacks from voting. Some whites had the audacity to say black people did not want to vote. It was not that they did not want to vote, but they didn't want to face the consequences for trying. Whites had not given up telling blacks that if they tried to vote they would lose their jobs. This strategy was a continuation of what had been told to blacks before to keep them from trying to vote.

Chapter 17

MY EDUCATION

I finished high school and completed two years of college. After finishing junior college, I went to a black university farther south. In 1963, I was beginning my junior year. At that time, it seemed that everything bad had happened that could happen. It did not seem that things could get worse, but they did. My mother subscribed to a newspaper which was full of things that were going on concerning racial issues. With the sit-ins and demonstrations that had begun in the summer of 1963, blacks were faced with violent acts inflicted on them by whites. The white people threw pepper in black people's eyes who were participating in the sit-ins. They sprayed them with paint and students who were participating were not allowed to sing any movement songs. When they did, they were beaten. The whites blamed Medgar Evers because they felt that he was a leader and that if they could stop him, they could put a stop to the movement.

Evers believed in what he was fighting for and just like Martin Luther King, Jr., he was not afraid of dying. He was quoted as saying at an NAACP rally that "Freedom has never been free." He went on to say that he loved his wife and his children with all of his heart, and that he would gladly die if that would make it better for them. A week before Evers' death, the Governor of Alabama was elected on June 11, 1963. In his inaugural speech, his historical words were, "Segregation now, segregation tomorrow, segregation forever." In order to initiate his famous words, he stood in the door of the University of Alabama to prevent two black students from entering the building, but because of federal officers his intent was to no avail.

There was so much unrest especially in the southern states. Crisis on top of crisis continued to happen. Whites still thought that Evers was the source of their troubles and they wanted him dead. Surely enough about a week after the inauguration, Evers was shot around midnight as he entered his home. The man that shot him went on trial, was exonerated, and later ran for a political position.

As if enough had not already happened, to top it all off, six months later after the death of Evers and the inauguration of the Governor, on November 22, 1963, the 35th President of the United States of America was assassinated as he rode in a motorcade in downtown Dallas, Texas. I will never forget that day as long as I live. I was 19 years old and in my junior year in college. I was in class when we were told that the President of the United States had been shot and had died. All classes were cancelled and we were sent to our dormitories. We actually sobbed. We did not know what was going to happen. That day was a day of sadness that affected the whole nation and was darker than a dozen midnights.

I had heard many times throughout my young life from people who did not live in the south but would come from the north to visit refer to the southern states, and especially Mississippi, as the "Sovereign State". For some who were visiting the state for the first time and faced prejudices, they were not able to understand how people could be so inhumane that they would kill adults and even children because of the color of their skin. Neither could we, who lived in the state, yet we had no voice. If anyone tried to rise up and go against the status quo, they were beaten or killed. It was as if saying, "If we keep them divided we can always conquer." Black Americans were upset and even angry about the killings that were going on in the south. It was more devastating when innocent children who knew no hatred were killed; children who loved not because of the color of their skin, but loved because they knew nothing else. These children, like any children, could not protect themselves and would not hurt a fly let alone a human being.

On Sunday, September 15, 1963, four little innocent girls who were attending church at the Seventh Street Baptist Church in Birmingham, Alabama were killed when someone bombed the church. These little girls were in church to worship the Lord and someone decided to bomb the church. This tactic was used to further intimidate black people in the south.

My mother wrote to me and told me to be careful because anything could happen because of the color of my skin. I was away at college when all of this happened. The college that I attended was an all-black college. I do not remember us having security guards at the entrance gate, but I do know that one would have to come through the gates to get on campus. We were blessed that as well as I can remember, we never had any racial incidents.

Now back home in my community, people were still watching over their children and keeping them as close to home as possible. For those of us who were away from home, they kept us in their prayers. People were still not venturing too far from home. When we left the university campus, we had to be taken from campus by bus to a town 21 miles away where we caught the Greyhound busses to go to our homes. When we went home for holidays and when school was out, we no longer had to sit at the back of the Greyhound busses coming home. Some years before, Rosa Parks, a black woman who due to a very trying day, got on the bus and sat in the back seats where blacks were allowed to sit. Then a white man got on the bus but all of the seats in the "white only" area were taken. He demanded that Rosa get up and give him her seat. She refused to do so and for this brave act she was arrested. This act was a step into unchartered waters. Everyone, especially in the southern states, was used to white people being able to sit wherever they chose to, regardless of whether it was a white or black section.

This act brought blacks together in a civil action called a "boycott". They now refused to use any public transportation to get wherever they were going. They walked or carpooled to get where they were going. This brought about a change to segregated public transportation. When going home from school on the busses, we did not have to go to the back of the busses; but our parents told us not to "rock the boat". They told us to still go to the back. They felt that our state was not ready to abide by the ruling that had outlawed segregation on public transportation. We did see some black people get on the busses and not go to the back. When they sat down, if looks could have killed them they would have died in their seats.

Sometimes during these trying times it just did not seem worth the effort to stay in the south to get an education when it seemed that educated blacks were not going anywhere in this state. It seemed if you did graduate from college all of the jobs that would pay anything were given to whites. So if you wanted to make any money you had to leave the south.

As I thought about the situations surrounding me, I have my mother to thank. She always said "Try to be the best you can, and if you try and try hard enough you will succeed." My mother was talking from experience. She planted within me the seed of faith, my teachers watered it by encouraging me to reach for the stars, and God increased within me the knowledge to believe that I could be whatever I wanted to be by His grace and mercy.

I gave great thought to the things that were going on around us. I knew that I was going on with my education and I was not going to let anything stand in my way of getting it. I loved my mother with all my heart and I never wanted to let my mother down. When I was growing up there were girls getting married on Sunday and going to the cotton field with their husband on Monday. I knew that this was not for me. I was not listening to those boys who wanted to whisper "sweet nothings" in your ear that did not amount to a hill of beans. I was going to make my mother proud of me because she had labored for the well-being of me and my brothers.

I graduated in 1964 with a Bachelor of Arts degree in Business Education. I wanted to get a degree in Business Administration, because I had no desire to teach school but my mother would not let me. She said that I could always be sure of getting a job and that I would love teaching school. My desire was to become a secretary, wear my beautiful dresses and high heel shoes, look good and smell good at work, and of course do my work. I had seen white women leaving their office jobs dressed in beautiful dresses and suits and their high heel shoes. They looked so nice and they looked like no matter how hot it was, they always looked cool and seemingly smelled good. I wanted to smell good, dress good, and look like I had never sweated a day in my life. I laugh about those days because when you are young you can be foolish and in desperate need of parental guidance.

Chapter 18

MOTHER WANTED SCHOOL FOR ME

I moved to the midwest region after graduating from college. My first job was a secretarial position where I worked for a year. It was not as glamorous and fulfilling as I had thought. I left that position to work as a substitute teacher for a year. Since there were no openings in my major I got a teaching position at the Job Corps Center. After a while, a position opened in my field in the local school district. I applied for it and was able to get back into the city. I was driving 60 miles a day round trip to the Job Corps Center. I worked for the school district until I retired. My mother was so proud of me. I made her happy because she said that I had been successful and her work of putting me through undergraduate school was not in vain.

One day while we were talking, she told me that one of her brothers had said it would be a waste of money to send me to college. I really do believe that it was her brother, Uncle Myers, because no one can make me believe that it was Uncle Troy, Uncle Jessie, or Mother's baby brother. She would never tell me who said it. She went to her grave with that secret. The only thing that I regret is that my mother did not live to see me get my Master's degree and my Educational Specialist degree. I wanted to get my Doctorate degree because I was so close, but our daughter was in college and we both could not go to school at the same time. I gave up my dream to give her a chance to fulfill hers which did not materialize.

During the summer of 1972, Mother came to spend that summer with my husband and me. I had no idea what she had gone through when we were younger and before I had started college. I asked her one day while we were talking about her life and her struggles, why she allowed Uncle Myers to treat us like he did? She started to cry as if someone had hit her. She told me that no one knew what she had to endure to raise us. She began to tell me things that she had kept embedded in her heart all of those years and had not shared with anyone. She was mistreated by her brother Myers. My mother was an easy going, soft spoken woman. People could treat her any way and she would never say a word.

After Papa died, Uncle Myers became what could have been called the master of the plantation. After I was old enough to see how he operated, it was like no one knew anything about running the farm except him. He thought that he knew everything and he would become angry if you asked him any questions about the farm. Mother said that when she was not in school she would go to the field. My two brothers, me, and my mother when she could, worked right along with our family in the field, but the money for our winter clothes did not come from our working in the field. As we have looked back over this incident for years, we may have not received money for our labor or to buy clothes, but thank God we learned how to work.

After the winter session of school was over, my mother did not get any money until the summer session started. After the summer session was over, she did not get any money until the winter session began again. Since my mother was not teaching school between these sessions, she needed to do some type of work to take care of us. She worked as a maid for a white woman who lived in town. She washed, ironed, cleaned the house, waxed the floors, and with a rag she mopped the kitchen floor on her hands and knees because this woman did not want her to use the mop. This woman that Mother worked for had lots of books in a special room. Mother said that she was dusting in this room one day and she stopped to look in a book. The woman saw her and the next time Mother dusted in that room all of the books had been moved. Mother said that this did not bother her because she needed the money for herself and her children.

I always thought that Mother paid cash for my clothes and my brothers' clothes. I did not know that my mother had to buy some of our shoes and clothes on credit because she did not have enough money to pay cash for all of them. I knew that she taught school and I thought she made a lot of money. I did not know that during the time that Mother taught school, teachers did not make much money. Mother was not living at home for free. She had to help buy food and help out in other ways. Farmer's crops had to be made and sold before there would be any money. Mother was glad to help in any way she could. In the winter, when it was time to buy our clothes, my mother paid whatever cash she had available for them because she did not have all of the money to pay for the clothes. Nonetheless, this did not stop us from getting any clothes. We grew each year and had to be clothed from top to bottom. My mother was a wonderful woman. God always blessed her to be able to get the things we needed.

Grandmother got whatever Uncle Myers gave her and she used part of that money to buy clothes for the two grandsons she was raising. Aunt Clare did hair so she was able to make a little money for herself. My Uncle Jessie and his wife and their children who were old enough worked in the field. Uncle Myers would work them very hard and talk to Uncle Jessie like he was not human; but Uncle Jessie would not say a thing. He was the kindest man I have ever known. Uncle Myers would do mean things to Uncle Jessie and say ugly things. Because Uncle Jessie and his wife had 13 wonderful children, Uncle Myers said they were like two dogs having puppies. What he did not know that in years to come, those children whom he referred to as puppies would be the ones who helped to take care of him, his wife, and his terminally ill son.

Uncle Myers would tell us that we were the laziest bastards he had ever seen. He would tell us that his son could work circles around us. He made his son feel that he was superior and that we could never live up to his high standards. There was nothing that we could do or say but endure whatever he said or did to us. If we had the courage to say something back to him he would have whipped us or talked about whipping us. If we were hoeing the cotton and his son got tired, he would let him get on the tractor and do some plowing. Uncle Myers would sometimes come to the field and do some work. When he did, we would chop the rows of cotton as fast as we could to make him tired. The moment we saw him pull off his cap, look up at the sun, and scratch his head, we knew we had him and we would be going home to eat dinner soon. There were times when he had to work on some of the farm equipment (so he said), and he could not come to the field. When he was there in the field with us, he never had anything nice to say to us.

Uncle Jessie could hoe a row of cotton faster than anyone I had ever seen. He was always kind to us but he made us work hard. When we were in the field with him, and that seemed to be always, we thought that we were never going to quit and go home for dinner. Sometimes he would tell us that we were going to make another round then we would stop. When we got that round done, we would do another, then we would go home to eat. I used to sometimes stand up, leaning on the handle of my hoe and I would be looking into the future. Uncle Jessie would say, "Come on **L.S.**" He did not know that I was looking way into the future dreaming of getting an education, a good job, living in a home somewhere way away from my hometown with air conditioning, and many, many trees around the house to keep me cool. When we left the field, we were hot, sweaty, tired, hungry, and thirsty.

Uncle Myers had a little store but when we came from the field hot and thirsty, did he offer to give us a cold pop that cost only five cents? No, never! There were times when Grandmother or Mother would send us to the store for an item. Uncle Myers would be behind the meat counter cutting himself a piece of cheese and eating it with crackers or vanilla wafers. He never asked us if we wanted a small piece of anything. He would just stand there before us and eat his cheese and never offer us a crumb of anything. He would give his dog a piece of food and never pay us any attention. This dog was more privileged than we were and had never worked a day in its life. When Uncle Myers was through doing what he was doing, he would get what we came to the store for. He took his own good time before he waited on us.

His actions seemed to say that he did not need us, we needed him. If we went to the store and the store was closed while he was listening to a baseball game, he would curse like a heathen before opening the store to let us in. Sometimes he would not bother to open the store. He never got in a hurry to do anything. Whenever our mother sent us to the store to get an item or two, she would send the money if she had it or she would ask him to put it on her bill. During the summer months after school was out, Mother would charge the small items she bought at the store so that she could put aside as much of the money as possible from working as a maid to help pay on our clothes for the winter. She never charged more items at Uncle Myer's store than she could afford to pay for later.

I remember one cold November morning, Mother and I were walking to town. It was three and a half miles from where we lived. We had on our scarves and coats but the wind was blowing right through our threadbare coats. I kept hearing my mother say something and I would ask her what she was saying. She would say "Nothing," but she kept doing this all the way to town. I later found out that she was praying. She was praying that the store owners would let her buy some of our clothes on credit (the ones that she did not have all of the money to pay for), so that we would have shoes and warm clothes for the winter. Although we had worked in the field and helped everyone else get clothes and shoes, Mother did not get any to help to pay for our or her clothes and shoes. We labored for free. In later years, I learned it was a blessing to labor for free because from this incident we learned that we could make it by the grace of God whether we received money or not.

Uncle Myers was the one that got what they called "the furnish". I do not know why it was called that. I never knew if the furnish was money borrowed but he got the money and he was to divide it equally between his mother, his brother, Jessie, and himself. Uncle Jessie and Grandmother did not get their equal share, but they managed with what they were given. He never told them why he kept the larger amount for himself and they never said anything to him about what he was doing.

Grandmother as well as other people in the community knew how to take a little and make it meet their needs. I remember when Uncle Jessie and Grandmother used to go to this little meat market that sat near 61 highway to buy hams. I do not remember the name of the market but they sold whole hams. These hams would be covered with something that looked like white fuzzy mold. This meat smelled bad to us, but it was needed to help out until butchering time. We used to hate seeing Grandmother and Uncle Jessie coming with those ugly smelling hams. They would cut enough meat from these hams to make a meal. Before the meat could be cooked, it had to be soaked in soda and water. We ate the meat because we had no choice.

CHAPTER 19

ALEX

Since Uncle Myers and Aunt Annabelle owned the little store in our neighbor, they ate meat every day. When Grace and I would go over to their house after they had eaten breakfast, there was always left over bacon or sausage and biscuits in a plate on the stove. We were afraid to ask for the leftover food. Sometimes Aunt Annabelle would ask if we wanted to eat the food. We would say yes, and she would tell us to eat it. We were not hungry when we went over there. Whatever we had eaten at home for breakfast was more than enough to fill us up. I think what we really wanted was the meat. We did not eat meat every day because our parents could not afford it. Their son, Alex would act like he did not want us to have the food even though he was not going to eat it. If his parents were not around us and we were over there, he would watch us like a hawk and tell us not to steal anything. He would have candy and money lying around and acted like he was waiting for us to steal it. When Uncle Myers was around, we knew that he could not help but overhear what his son was saying to us. He would sit there with a homemade rolled cigarette hanging from his bottom lip looking under-eyed at us and would not say a word.

They all saved a small amount of money, but they especially saved dimes in large jars and the jars were in various places throughout the house.

One day $10 in dimes were missing from the home of Uncle Myers and Aunt Annabelle. No one knew exactly what happened to the dimes. They could only speculate that since our cousin of 13 sisters and brothers had gone over to play, he got the dimes. He told his father, his Uncle Myers and Aunt Annabelle that he saw the dimes but he did not take them. Uncle Myers and his family said that Lenny was not welcome in their home anymore because he could not be trusted. For the sake of Uncle Myers and his family, Uncle Jessie whipped his son even though he did not believe his son had taken the dimes. Sometime later he found that his son had been telling the truth all along. It was not his son, but his nephew who had the dimes.

The boy that was not to be successful in life went on to become a highly thought of and a successful man married with children. He spent over 20 years in the U.S. Army, built he and his family a nice home on the home place and furnished it with beautiful furniture from Germany. He retired from the U.S. Army with a very good retirement and benefits. After retiring, he came home and got hired on the police force as second in command; a position many years before would not have been given to a black man. Uncle Myers and Aunt Annabelle wanted him to come over and visit them now that he had not failed in life as they thought he would. He would not go over there. They said that if you were not a policeman, he did not want to be bothered with you but that was not the case. When someone has thought the worst of you and mistreated you, you may forgive but you do not forget. Alex told me out of his own mouth in July, 2007, when he was terminally ill and near death that Lenny would not come to see him. I could understand why, but I made no comment.

Now that the truth had come to the forefront, would anyone believe that this same incident could happen again? Yes, to everyone's dismay it did happen again. This time it was a female cousin, Alyssa, who had gone over to our uncle and aunt's home not to play, but to clean it.

While over there cleaning, she was accused of taking $10 dollars in dimes. She also tried to clear her name because she knew that she did not do anything wrong. My aunt, Aunt Annabelle, went over to Uncle Jessie and Aunt Abbey's house and told them that Alyssa had taken some of their dimes. Again, to keep the peace between his family and his brother's family, Alyssa was whipped for something she did not do.

Look how high God can lift you above the lies, slander, and meanness inflicted upon you by those who try to destroy you.

It is bad to raise your child or children to feel that they are far better and smarter than anyone else, and that they will definitely succeed in life whereas every other child is going to fail because you think your child has more to offer. Be careful of what you do or say about other people's children because it will certainly come back someday to haunt you. One thing that has stayed with me and that I learned as a child and in later years as an adult is that the truth will prevail, it will set you free, and it will not destroy your character nor set a stumbling block in your way.

Alex has four lovely children by three different wonderful young ladies, two of whom I know personally. He could have possibly married any one of them, supported all of his children, and whomever he married. He would have had the opportunity to watch the children take their first step, see their first smile, and speak their first word. At first Uncle Myers and Aunt Annabelle did not acknowledge the children as their grandchildren. When they did finally acknowledge three of them, they were old enough to not fret over whether they were or were not accepted. The mothers of these children did a fantastic job of raising them.

One day we were all gathered at Uncle Myer's house after the funeral of Aunt Annabelle. We were sitting around the dining room table and Alex came in with a young lady and told his father that this young woman was his daughter and she was Uncle Myer's granddaughter. We thought that he would say something to the child, but he did not open his mouth. He just looked at her. I had never seen her before. We thought that it was horrible the way he treated her. Alex always said that if he ever got married he would marry the young woman who gave birth to his first two children. She was a friend that we had known for years. He said if he did not marry her, he was not going to marry anyone because he loved her. Why he did not marry her years before when he was in good health is beyond us.

One summer when I was at home visiting my grandmother and my Aunt Clare, (my mother had already passed away); Alex was there visiting his parents, too. He and I talked at length about his wanting to marry this one young woman. I asked him what was keeping him from marrying her. She had given birth to his son and daughter, but he would never say why he would not go ahead and marry her. As he talked, I really believe that his parents had something to do with it. They always felt that he was better than anyone and I really believe that he gave up his own happiness to please his parents. He did marry this young woman but they only lasted a little over three months as husband and wife. She made him a good wife. But he did not treat her like a husband should treat his wife. I have never heard her say an unkind word about him or anything against him even after his death. Shortly before Alex's death, my husband and I were leaving for home the next day so I went over to talk to him. I told him that he had a good woman and he should treat her right. I said if it were not for her he would be in a nursing home, because Uncle Jessie's children could not take him to his doctor appointments every time he had one. He was terminally ill and could not drive. I also told him that this young woman had her own home which he was able to visit and see that she did not need what he had. She came because she had loved him all of her life and he was the father of her children. Everything that he had was sunk in debt. He did not have anything to leave her without a cost attached to it. When he married this young woman, she stood by him until he drew his last breath. I think she is a remarkable woman and was a good wife and mother. The other young women who had children by him are remarkable young women and good mothers as well.

Another summer, years before Alex became ill, we were all at home. We all used to come home around the Fourth of July every year to celebrate our grandmother's birthday. This particular summer, my cousin Grace and I had walked over to visit Aunt Annabelle and Uncle Myers. Alex was there but he had not made it down to the home place. He had been in his hangout for a whole day and night and had not made it home to see his parents. Night caught us over to Aunt Annabelle and Uncle Myer's house and we were afraid to walk back over to Uncle Jessie's house. There were no street or yard lights and it was very dark. Aunt Annabelle said that she would walk us part the way home. As we were walking, she caught my and Grace's hand and said that we, her nieces and her nephews, were going to have to take care of her and Uncle Myers because if we did not do it, they would have no one to look after them. When they began to age and fell into bad health, it was the nieces and nephews, which were Uncle Jessie's children, who took care of them not because they had to but out of the goodness of their hearts. Uncle Myers would have rather died than say that they made a mistake in the way they raised Alex.

I often wondered if they ever gave any thought to the way they mistreated people. I really believe that Aunt Annabelle was afraid of Uncle Myers and did a lot of things out of fear. He talked about her and even cursed her. Alex saw a lot of things that they did. If you mistreat people or try to beat them out of things that belong to them, and your children see you doing this, you can pass this trait on to your own child or children.

Many people in the neighborhood had accounts at our uncle and aunt's store. They had a screened-in cage that sat on the counter. They kept an account book that held the names and amounts that people owed them. One day I was in the store with my mother. She wanted to pay some on her account. Aunt Annabelle went behind the counter, got the book, and said that she was adding up the amount Mother owed. Mother said she could see her and she was not adding *up* her account, but she was adding *to* the account. When she came from behind the counter, she showed Mother the amount she owed. Mother told her that she had not taken that much up on credit and that she must have made a mistake. Mother said that she would write down what she bought on credit each time she charged anything. She went into her purse, found the list of what items were bought and the amount of each item. Mother said that Aunt Annabelle's eyes almost popped out of her head. She told Mother that she must have gotten her account mixed up with someone else's account. My mother said she wondered how many people had accounts there and did not notice how much they had charged and when it was time to pay, they paid double the amount actual owed.

This incident was not the end of Aunt Annabelle's escapades. One year, we were through picking cotton, but there were bolls of cotton that did not open in time to be picked when all the other cotton was picked. Uncle Myers said that Aunt Abbey and Aunt Clare could have the cotton if they picked it. There were enough bolls filled with cotton to make a bale of cotton. It was coming up to Christmas and they were going to use the money from the cotton to buy their Christmas presents. Aunt Clare and Aunt Abbey, along with several of Aunt Abbey's children helped pick the bale of cotton. The cotton was sold and they got $120 for that bale of cotton. They divided it and each got $60. They tried to get Aunt Annabelle to help them, but she said she had to take care of the store and could not help them.

After getting the money, Aunt Abbey said she was going in the store and pay off her bill which she said was only a few dollars. Aunt Clare told her to wait until after Christmas since this was their Christmas money and they were going to go shopping. Aunt Abbey told Aunt Clare that the amount was only a few dollars and she would have some money left to use for shopping. Aunt Clare said she went in the store with her and Aunt Abbey asked to pay her bill. Aunt Annabelle went behind the counter and got her account book, added up the amount and told Aunt Abbey that she owed $60.

She took all of Aunt Abbey's money. Aunt Clare said that Aunt Annabelle did not want to help them, but she believed until her dying day that Aunt Annabelle intended to take Aunt Abbey's money. Aunt Clare said that she knew Aunt Annabelle was not going to mess with her because she would get a good cursing out. She said that Aunt Abbey came out of that store with tears in her eyes.

It is hard to believe some of the things that happened to us, but as hard as it is to believe - they did happen. Over the years when we have gathered for family occasions or talked on the phone we have often remembered and talked about the things that happened.

Once we were on our way to the field. We had some land called the "New Ground." Why it was called the New Ground we do not know. There was a dirt road that we had to travel to get to this piece of land. It was surrounded by woods with no homes or anything that was visible. It was so miserably hot. The wind seemed to stay at the top of the trees and never came down to the ground where we could have a bit of it even though it was hot wind. If it had come below the tree tops, some wind would have been better than none.

This particular day Uncle Jessie was driving us to the field and Grandmother was in the truck with him. All of the children were on the back of the truck along with Mother and Aunt Abbey. They were sitting at the very back of the truck with their feet hanging off the back. Uncle Jessie hit a bump in the road and Aunt Abbey fell off. She was pregnant at the time. We began hitting on the cab of the truck, but Uncle Jessie did not stop. He thought we were playing. Aunt Abbey was laying on the ground laughing. Mother jumped off of the truck to see about her. When she saw that Aunt Abbey was alright she began to laugh, too. We began to beat harder on the cab of the truck and scream. Uncle Jessie stopped and got out of the truck to find out what was going on. When he saw what had happened he immediately went to see about Aunt Abbey. Mother had gotten up and went to her also. Aunt Abbey had sat up but she was still laughing. She said she saw Mother jump off of the truck and all she could see through the dust was her skirt above her knees and two little legs sticking up in the air. Mother began laughing again when she saw that Aunt Abbey was alright. She said that Aunt Abbey had the strangest look on her face when Uncle Jessie hit that bump and she fell off of the truck.

Chapter 20

NEW GROUND

This particular day, Aunt Annabelle, Uncle Myers, nor Alex was with us. Uncle Myers said he had to work on equipment, Alex had to plow, and Aunt Annabelle had to take care of the store. When we quit for dinner, we came by their house and we saw Aunt Annabelle get up off the bed where she was taking a nap. No one was plowing nor working on equipment.

We were all glad when we finished with the New Ground. We did not have a cooler to take water in nor ice to put in a cooler. We would get so thirsty that someone would have to walk about a fourth of a mile to Uncle Troy and Aunt Paisley's house, get water in a molasses bucket, and bring it back to us so that we could quench our thirst.

We continued to grow, work hard, and have our dreams about our futures. I do not think any of us dreamed of becoming farmers because none of us became one. As we grew, things were still going on in the southern states pertaining to race relations. Our parents were still trying to shield us from bad things which were still happening. Some things were so bad that they could not be hidden especially when it happened to someone in our community.

One day a young man in our community was killed. What a sad day! Aunt Clare had seen this young man on the Saturday before his death. He was dressed nicely and was on his way into town. While walking to town, he stopped and talked to my aunt for a little while. She said she told him to be careful. She did not know that she was talking to him for the last time. He was well known in our community. My mother had taught him when he was a boy.

After he did not show up for several days everyone began to wonder what could have happened to him. A week later, they found his body on the side of the road in a nearby town. Someone had killed him. He had been seen by several white people who said that he was entertaining some white people in a white club who had been drinking and was having him dance for them. It was on a Sunday when his body was found. Everyone in the community was in a state of shock. On this sad day in our community, there were no words to describe how everyone was feeling about this young man's death. We had to stay even closer to home where our parents could keep a watchful eye on us. To us, as children, it was very frightening.

We continued to grow and to work hard, but there was still trouble lurking in the dark that was again going to traumatize our community. One of our neighbors had a little girl. Everyone talked about how happy she was because she wanted a girl. One day she left the field to go and nurse the baby. After nursing her, she went back to the field. The baby was asleep when she went back to the field. There were older children in the house but it was thought that the older children went to sleep and somehow the baby got out of the house. The baby was crawling at this time. After leaving work for the day, the neighbor went to get her baby and could not find her. People began to think that maybe the baby had not been asleep when she left, crawled out of the bed, saw the way her mother went, and was trying to follow her. They thought that there was a possibility that the baby lost her way and crawled into the woods. People got flash lights and lanterns to comb the woods looking for her. They looked in little streams of water but no baby was found.

After a week of searching and the baby was not found, the search was called off. People thought, as sad as it was and the hurt seen on the mother's face, the baby was probably dead. One of our neighbors said that he heard a baby crying in the woods. He got up one dark night with a flash light in one hand, a gun in the other hand and went into the woods where he thought he heard the sound of a crying baby, but he did not find anything. My mother would not let us go very far from home to visit friends because it was too dangerous. Other parents kept their children close as well.

There was high water from a lake located near our community. There were a lot of wooded areas. People were saying that there were panthers, bears, and hyenas in this area. Some said they had heard them. Others said they had seen them. So much was being said that no one knew what to believe.

Because of the high water, it was believed that these animals had left and were looking for higher ground to get away from the water. Maybe one of these animals had come into our area where the baby had crawled and had eaten her. There were still other sightings. A man said he was walking home one night and he saw a wild man and maybe it got the baby. Some thought maybe because the baby was black it was killed by someone white. There were many speculations, but no answers. It is amazing that we grew up as normal children after enduring so many horrific things in our lives, but thank God we did.

About three months after the baby had been missing, one of our neighbors said that his dog had been coming to the house with a foul odor on his breath. He did not know what it was because dogs in the country could find dead animals to eat. After about a year, this same dog brought a small human skull to the house. When our neighbor saw the skull, he knew immediately that it had to be the baby's skull. The sheriff was called and some of the other neighbors began to search the area. They found the bones of the baby and the little dress which she had been wearing was almost destroyed. How this baby got that far from the house where her mother left her for the last time, the community did not know. They never did find out as far as we knew. There were many speculations, but there was never any solid evidence to convict anyone.

Chapter 21

MOTHER AND I

Mother and I sat on the porch of my home every day and talked. It was fun to sit out there with her. As she talked, I was busily taking notes. Mother and I would not be in a hurry. We would cook dinner early and this gave us a chance to spend a lot of time talking about everything. My husband would come home from his job at the General Motors plant. We would eat dinner and he would go to his second job where he worked as an umpire for the sports league. Sometimes Mother and I would ride over to the park where he was umpiring a game and watch him work. Most evenings we stayed home and I listened to her talk. I always took notes about the things she was sharing with me. After I had listened to the struggles, hard times, and abuse my mother had gone through and how she had come out victorious, I told her that I was going to write a book about her life. She laughed and said, "There is not anything exciting about my life, but I want to read it." I started writing this book over 40 years ago, but did not finish it until 28 years after my mother's death.

My mother lived and breathed education. It was her whole world other than God, her children, and her family members. My mother did not have to depend on any man, other than God, to help her. Her desire was that I also get an education and she was not going to stand for anything else. I could not see it then, but I have been wonderfully blessed because of her wisdom and leadership in being able to direct me in the right direction to know the importance of getting an education and persevering until I had gotten my Bachelor of Science degree in Business Education. After my mother's death, I received my Master's degree and an Educational Specialist degree in Administration. I am grateful to my mother who, by example, helped me to be where I am today.

As I have often remembered after I had finished high school and it was time for me to go to college, my mother said I would be going to our local junior college. It was located across the street from the high school where I had graduated. I did not want to go there. I wanted to go out of town but Mother said no indeed. She knew that I did not need that much freedom. In later years, I realized that I needed to be near where she could keep my feet on the ground, see that I had chosen the right type of friends, monitor my behavior, see that I was doing my school work, keep me focused, and teach me how to look beyond today into the future.

My mother was still teaching school and working for this white woman on weekends so that she would have enough money to pay my tuition. Her school sessions were not divided into two sessions anymore. Schools were now in session for nine months but sometimes she had to borrow money. I will never forget that there were two people in our community who had told my mother if she ever needed money to pay my tuition they would lend it to her because they wanted to see me make it in school. It was said that these two people had plenty of money. They both were the ones who came to my mother and told her if there was anything they could do to keep me in school they would be happy to do it. Sometimes mother did have to borrow money for some of my tuition when she did not have it all. She would always pay them back. They never talked about her borrowing money from them. Mother said that her neighbor's husband never said a word to her that was not becoming to a woman.

There was also a white family that played a part in my education. They owned a small chicken farm. They would pay me to gather eggs and sometimes I took care of their first grandchild. They were a nice white couple. I remember one Saturday I had been working for them and it was lunch time. She fixed my plate on the table in the dining room. I picked up my plate and was heading to the kitchen. She asked where I was going and I said in the kitchen. She and her husband both told me that I was not going to eat in the kitchen and that I was going to sit at the table with them. I did not know what to say. I could not remember any black person sitting and eating at the same table as the white people they were working for. They paid me well and I was able to help my mother with some of my expenses. I must say that they were very good to me. They helped with my education by providing some work for me. I will never forget them.

Before school started and I was about to enter my second year of junior college, I still needed work so I again worked for the same couple on Saturday. People were hiring other people to chop cotton. We were also chopping cotton on what we called our farm. I had asked my mother to let me chop cotton on another farm for two or three weeks so I could make some money to buy some clothes, a pair of shoes, notebooks, paper, pens, pencils, and other things I was going to need when school started. She told me that I could. I chopped cotton for these people. They had some land right next to Uncle Myer's field. Mother and I did not know that Uncle Myers was going to get mad and start cursing at my mother to make her bring me back to what I called his farm. My mother said that he got very angry with her. She told him that she did not have all of the money for me to start my second year in college. He told Mother that he did not give a damn because I was not going to be anything anyway. He said that he was not going to pay a dime to help me. I do not know what gave him this idea. I had never done anything to give him a reason to believe I would not be anything. Years before, when I was much younger and was chopping cotton, I stopped and was leaning on my hoe handle dreaming of making something out of myself. I wanted to have a good job, live in a nice home with trees around it, and have air conditioning to keep the house cool on the inside. He never did give my mother one red cent to help defray the cost of my education or my brother next to me, but we still had to work in the fields so that he would have money and could eat meat every day and pay for his son to go to college (which he did not give a hoot about because he stayed only one year). Yes, he still gave Uncle Jessie and Grandmother money after the crops had been gathered and sold, but he was not fair. He still kept the larger amount for himself. It took time for Grandmother and Uncle Jessie to find out what he was doing, but when they did they were both still so kind and forgiving. They never demanded that he give them their equal share. Why they did not confront him is still beyond my understanding.

One time Uncle Myers and Aunt Annabelle sold a bale of cotton without anyone in the family knowing about it. There's an old saying that says, "What goes on in the dark will eventually come to the light." That is true. Somehow it was found out what they had done. Uncle Myers must have been doing a lot of things because when it was found out, he was about to cause the family to lose the land that Papa had bought. This was family land and Grandmother had said Papa did not want any white man telling his family that it was time for them to go to the field. Uncle Myers was so busy doing wrong that he had signed all of the land over to Uncle Jessie. When Uncle Jessie and someone else (I believe it was Mother's baby brother) met with the lawyer, this was when it was discovered that Uncle Myers had sold cotton and kept the money for himself. It was also learned that when Aunt Abbey's mother, who worked for a very wealthy white family found out that the land was about to be lost, she talked to her employer and asked him to take over the financial notes on the land so that it would not be lost. She did not want to see her daughter, husband, and grandchildren looking for a place to live. From the crops made each year, the employer who took over the notes on the land would be paid in installments until the whole amount owed to him would be paid.

Uncle Myers tried to say that he did not do it. The lawyer told him to shut up, because he was lying. I guess you could say that he was backed into a corner, had no way out, and it was known that he was the only one who could have done this. He handled all of the money and he was the one who gave Grandmother and Uncle Jessie their money. He found out that day that he had signed all of the land over to Uncle Jessie and did not know that he had done it. The lawyer told Uncle Jessie if he was him, he would not sign over to Uncle Myers a foot of land. Uncle Jessie, being the kind man that he was, said that Uncle Myers was his brother and he signed the land back over to him.

Uncle Jessie and Aunt Abbey had worked hard in the fields all of their lives. I believe that Aunt Abbey worked herself to death. She died at an early age. She was 54 years old when she died. She was still a young woman. She has children that have lived longer than she lived. They had a big family, but they stayed together through good times and bad time and they raised their children. They truly lived the part of the wedding vows which says, "Will you take this man/woman whom you now hold by the hand to be your lawfully wedded husband/wife? Will you love, honor, cherish, and obey; cleaving only unto him/her until by death shall you be separated?" Uncle Jessie and Aunt Abbey were separated only by her death. They raised 13 children whom they didn't have to get not one of them out of jail. They raised children who were hard workers. They were taught to have good work ethics because they saw them in their father and mother. Not all of Uncle Jessie and Aunt Abbey's children were grown when she died. She had Eugene and Jasmine living at home who stepped in and helped raise the sisters and brother who were still young when their mother died. I was grown and no longer lived at home when the last four of Uncle Jessie and Aunt Abbey's children were born. All 13 of their children were successful in their endeavors. From this family there are college graduates, a first vice president of a large bank, a retired service man, school secretary, managers of businesses, government workers, and other careers. These are the children that Uncle Myers tried to degrade. Uncle Jessie lived approximately ten years after Aunt Abbey died. She did not live to see that all of her children succeeded in life. Uncle Jessie got to see his children succeed. The children took good care of him just as they had done for their mother. When any of us would go home, we would always go to see Uncle Jessie before leaving. He would come to the car and talk to us before we left, and he always said he sure hated to see us leave. We knew that he was genuine and was not just saying something to make conversation. Some of his children who left home after growing up, marrying, and having children of their own, have returned to their birthplace and have homes of their own. Some retired, but decided to continue in the work force not because they had to, but because they wanted to.

We do not remember Uncle Jessie talking about anyone or saying that he did not like a person. We can remember when Alex would come home, he would come to Uncle Jessie's house or he would stay in Tunica for a day or two before going to his parent's house. His father or mother would not know that he was there. Alex said that after he was grown, his father would curse him and say unkind things to him. When he would come to Uncle Jessie's house, he would tell him that he should be ashamed of himself and that he needed to go see his parents. It could have been just as easy for Uncle Jessie to tell him what kind of man his father was and that he should never go see him. That was not like Uncle Jessie. If he could not help you, he was not going to do anything to hurt you.

I do not know what I would have done without Uncle Jessie when my mother died. That was the saddest day of my life. I guess I was in a state of shock and disbelief because I could not think. Uncle Jessie stood by me. He and Martin, my cousin, took me to pick out the grave, the casket, get the obituaries printed, and make arrangements for the funeral. After we had picked out the casket, I was so sad and hurt I began to cry. Uncle Jessie said, "Everything is going to be alright." **I w**as so glad that he and Marti**n went** with me to help take care of funeral arrangements. My mother thought the world of her brother Jessie. She once said that Jessie and I don't have any extra money, but we have a clear conscious. We can lay our heads on our pillows and sleep peacefully and not be tormented in our sleep because of doing mean and evil things.

When Uncle Jessie and Aunt Abbey's children were little, they all lived in a small house. When we were little and our mother was still living with our father, we lived in a smaller house than Uncle Jessie and his family. The house we lived in was called a "shotgun" house. It was called that because one could look through the front door of the house all the way to the back. Although Uncle Jessie and Aunt Abbey lived in a small house, Aunt Abbey kept the cleanest house of anyone we had ever known. We used to wonder how she kept a house as clean as she did with so many children. Now her children have followed in her footsteps.

Their houses are spotless. Not only are her daughters' homes clean, but her sons can clean a house as good as any woman. They can cook and decorate a house that would put some women to shame. Living in close quarters did not inhibit the children from becoming great achievers.

Mother said she knew their children were going to succeed. Uncle Jessie had instilled into the minds of his children just as she had instilled into the mind of me and my two brothers that if we stayed in school and got an education we could live better. My brother taught school and my baby brother worked for United Parcel Services. We all have found this principle to be true, if you stay in school and get an education, you can live better. We, who came from very low beginnings, have been able to reach the mountain top and have been able to see from whence we have come. It does not matter where you come from, whether you have your own bedroom, whether you buy your clothes from a name brand store or from a thrift store, or if you live in a big fine house. What does matter is that you know where you are going and have some ideas of how you are going to get there. That is important because it gives you something to strive for. Whether he knew it or not, Uncle Myers helped us to know that we would not always have to take his abuse. We knew the only way to get away from him was to use our time in school wisely to prepare ourselves for our future. Because of his abuse and being unkind to us, he planted the seeds of success in our lives and he did not know what he had done. We nurtured those seeds and helped them to grow with the help of our parents. Now we are reaping the benefits of those seeds - our success - which were planted and have grown in our lives.

Uncle Myers was not kind to his older brother Uncle Troy. Uncle Troy was kind hearted like Grandmother and Uncle Jessie. Uncle Myers would mistreat him in front of people at the store. People would talk about how he treated Uncle Troy. They wondered why he would treat his brother like he did. It seemed like Uncle Myers had no conscious. I can remember walking to Uncle Troy and Aunt Paisley's house to get Uncle Troy to give me a V-cut hair line in the back. In those days women wore V-lines. If it was done right it was very stylish. Uncle Troy always did a good job. Uncle Jessie and Uncle Troy had similar mannerisms in the way they treated people. We never saw or heard that they said anything unkind to people or tried to embarrass them in front of other people as Uncle Myers would do. As children, we used to wonder how Grandmother could have had a son like Uncle Myers who was so different from her other three sons.

Uncle Troy and Aunt Paisley had one girl and six boys. Their daughter, **Vanessa**, died when she was a baby. Uncle Troy's children, like Uncle Jessie's children were hard workers. They never had to go and bail any of their children out of jail. Each of their sons grew up to be men of good character and good husbands. Each was successful in their careers, provided, and still provides for their families. None of them have had to return home because they could not make it on their own in this world. Uncle Troy was Papa's oldest son. I had often wondered why he did not own part of the land that Papa bought. Uncle Troy's son, Junior, explained to me the reason Uncle Troy did not own part of the land. After giving thought to the reasons why, I do believe it was for the best because Uncle Myers would have made Uncle Troy's life miserable with his under handed dealings. Aunt Ava was the youngest of the girls. She and her husband moved to Chicago when they were young. They had five children. Two passed away. The children that are still living have done well in their endeavors. Aunt Ava's oldest son was raised by our grandmother but he has been successful, too. Aunt Ava never had any encounters with Uncle Myers because she did not live on the farm. If she had lived on the farm she would not have taken any of his foolishness. She would have set him on fire with words and would have never even laid a hand on him.

My mother's baby brother was the youngest of all of Papa and Grandmother's children. I don't think that Uncle Myers ever messed with his baby brother. I never knew of his living at home and neither can the other cousins. When we were older, we remembered him coming home with his family to visit us. We stood in awe of him when he visited because we had not grown up around him. He was kind, he was friendly, and I don't ever recall him saying anything unkind to us or to his children. I think that Uncle Myers was afraid to start anything with him. He was intelligent and was well informed about many issues. He was not a farmer and Uncle Myers had nothing to hold over his head. He had travelled and seen so many places and knew things that Uncle Myers had never seen and would never see or know. So we all believed

Uncle Myers thought it was best to not tangle with him because he was definitely not going to win.

We enjoyed our uncle, his wife, and their children although we did not grow up with them. When they came, they always had on shoes, socks, and nice clothes; but they played with us and did not pay any attention that we were as barefooted then as we were the day we were born. They paid no attention to that so we felt good about being around them. I will always be grateful to my aunt, my uncle's wife. At the age of twelve, she talked to me about life which my mother refused to talk to me about. At that age, I still believed that the woman who was a midwife had babies in her black medical bag. When Aunt Abbey and our Aunt Ava had a baby, we were sent away from the house, and the same was done for Aunt Abbey's children. When we returned to either of the homes, we found a baby was there. When we all were much younger, we tried to figure out how we could get the midwife's bag so we could see how many babies were in there. To this day I will never know why my mother did not talk to me about babies and how they were made. That subject was taboo even though she had given birth to us.

When we are able to get together it is wonderful to be around each other. We enjoy each other's company. We can each be proud of ourselves, because by the grace of God we were taught good work ethics and how to live by the values that we were taught. We still laugh and talk about Uncle Myers and the things that he did. It is amazing that we do not carry any hatred or hard feelings in our hearts against him and Aunt Annabelle. After we were grown and had left home he seemed to want us to be around him. We would go to see him but we did not spend a lot of time at his home. We still wondered why he was so different from Grandmother's other children. We were never able to find an answer to that question.

I thought to bring this up to Grandmother because now that I was grown I had to know and didn't fear being reprimanded. She said that Uncle Myers was the splitting image of Papa's brother Leonard. She said that he was just different from her other children. I wanted to know how they handled a child that was so different from the other siblings. I never got a chance to ask because God decided it was time for Grandmother to go be with the Lord.

Chapter 22

GRANDMOTHER GOES HOME

Our Grandmother died on June 17, 1990 at the age of 99. After her funeral, all of her grandchildren were sitting out in the front yard. We tried to remember if we had ever heard Grandmother talk about anyone or say anything unkind about or to anyone. None of us had ever heard her curse, talk about anyone, or say anything unkind to anyone. The next day after the funeral, which was Sunday, Uncle Myers came over to grandmother's house. My cousin Alyssa and I rode back over to his house with him. He began to talk about Grandmother and what he had said to her when he was a child ~~and~~ when she had bought him a pair of overalls. He began to shake his head from side to side as if he was going to have a seizure or had become possessed by a demonic spirit. He said he told Grandmother that he was not going to wear those damn overalls and as far as he was concerned, she could wear those damn things herself. Alyssa and I sat there and looked at him. We did not believe what he was saying because Papa was still living when Uncle Myers was a child. There was no way that Papa was going to let him talk to Grandmother like that and get away with it. He seemed to have enjoyed his own tale. While Alyssa and I were over there and after listening to him talk about what he had said, I could no longer sit there. Something seemed to have boiled over in my spirit and I told him how all of us had suffered and how he had treated us. I cannot remember all of his words, but I do know that he tried to justify that what he had done was to save the land and to help each of us to have an acre of land to build a house on if we wanted to come home. He did not have to be concerned with that issue. I do believe that those of us who are older and have not returned home will never return. We will always return for visits because we will always be like sisters and brothers because of our upbringing. While I released the feelings that I had held on to for years, Aunt Annabelle was sitting in the room with us and she got up and went outside. When Alyssa and I were leaving, she was chopping something in the yard with a hoe and she was crying. She knew that we had been mistreated and they were getting older and that they would need us long before any of us would need them.

After Grandmother died and was buried that fall, it was time to get Grandmother's part of the rent money. Uncle Myers and Uncle Jessie were no longer farming the land because we were all grown and gone so there was no one to work the land. Plus small farmers could not compete in farming because the big farmers were now using heavy equipment to farm the land. They did not have to use human labor like they had done once. The land that Papa bought for the family was now being rented out.

Aunt Clare called Uncle Myers when he gave her part of Grandmother's rent money and asked him for the other part of the money that he had given Grandmother. When she did this, he cursed her and told her that she and my mother, who had been dead at that time for six years, had never done a damn thing on the farm. When I was told this I could not believe what I was hearing. On the night that my mother died, when they came to the house to take her body away, he cried like a baby. He had trouble trying to breathe and Aunt Annabelle had to rush over to their home to get his medication. I could not believe that he had the nerve to talk about my mother. We had worked in her place and it was to no avail. He became so angry with Aunt Clare that he never came back to the house to see her or to see about her.

He completely stopped talking to her because she asked for the rest of Grandmother's rent money. He intended to keep that portion of the money for himself since his mother was dead. Aunt Clare deserved that money because she gave up her life to take care of their mother.

From that day until the day he died, Aunt Clare said he never put his foot in the house again. She said that sometimes she would be out in the front yard and he would be passing the house in his truck. He would look the other way to keep from speaking to her. This contemptuous attitude seemed to bathe itself in the Mississippi air.

When I think about my Uncle Myers's feud with my Aunt Clare, I always think about a place called Sugar Ditch because of what was hidden from the public. Uncle Myers was somewhat of a replica of Sugar Ditch because of all his hidden agendas and the things he kept hidden from his mother, brother, and his other family members. He presented himself to the public as a caring person, but underneath this caring persona was a mean man with an ugly disposition. As I recanted his behavior over the years, I equated him to Sugar Ditch because it was full of feces and so was Uncle Myers.

The history and the discovery of Sugar Ditch came after most of us were grown and had moved away. How do I think that my uncle's ways reminded me of this place? Well, he reminded me of Sugar Ditch because it seemed as if he did not care if others suffered, just as the people who created Sugar Ditch did not care about the people who ended up there. He wanted his needs met and did not care if other's needs were met beyond what they needed to survive. He was the judge and the jury. Sugar Ditch was a place located in a small town called Tunica, Mississippi. It was a quiet, peaceful town with its very clean Main street, which ran through the town with its manicured lawns cut and shaped to perfection with beautifully shaped trees. It had a clock which I had heard but had actually never seen that chimed on the quarter of the hour. It played spirituals every hour that helped to uplift the down trotted hearts and bring joy to the hearts of all who heard it.

The small, quiet, peaceful, clean town of Tunica, Mississippi, located approximately 37 miles south of Memphis, Tennessee and approximately 45 miles southeast of West Memphis, Arkansas made its national debut sometime during the late 80's. Its hidden agenda was exposed, just like my uncle's hidden agenda of his misleading endeavors.

When Tunica's horrific incident was exposed, it shocked the whole nation and put Tunica in the national spotlight. People could not believe that there was a place like Sugar Ditch in the United States of America - the richest country on Earth.

Chapter 23

1985 SUGAR DITCH DRIVE

Sugar Ditch got its distinct name because of the incident that happened there. The residents who lived on Sugar Ditch had once been very hard workers while living on white plantations. These people were replaced by heavy farm equipment that could triple the amount of work that an individual could do in a day. The machines did not get tired and they did not get sick. Because of their being displaced by heavy farm equipment, these people had no place to go or to lay their heads. There was absolutely no kind of work for all of them. There were only so many maid and janitorial jobs which were already taken. Jobs to keep the grass and shrubbery cut around the wealthy owners' homes, on the grounds of public buildings, the many behind-the-scene blacks cooking in white restaurants - many of these jobs were already taken.

These displaced people could not live on the streets so shacks without electricity were built for them using the poorest quality of material. What was so tragic about these shacks was that they were built where the town and home owners' raw sewerage ran right in front of their doors. They were inundated with the free flow of this filth, large rats, flies, and roaches. Where flies are, you can be assured that the flies' lava was abundant too and waiting to become little flies. It was hard for the residents to put into words the smell that they breathed in both day and night along with the combination of sweltering heat. Even when they sat at their tables to eat their meals, this odor seemed to mingle with the taste of their food and caused many to become nauseated. This place became nationally known as the infamous, "Sugar Ditch."

Sugar Ditch was not miles away hidden in some secluded area. It was only a few blocks from the neat, clean, and tidy rows of the downtown stores in Tunica. There were no indoor plumbing or facilities for these families. Some had very large containers that they used for their personal use and when these containers were full, they took the waste and emptied it into the ditch making the container ready to use when needed again. These conditions were not fit for an animal, but what could the people do? It was all they had.

There were a group of people who detested the conditions that poor blacks were living in. This group was instrumental in getting in touch with a well-known black leader who was president of an organization and he began to bring these conditions to the forefront so that the nations could see what was happening in Tunica. This leader was quoted as referring to this town as "The home of a cesspool called Sugar Ditch." He said that his organization would adopt the town, which he renamed "America's Ethiopia." This was said to allow congressmen and senators the opportunity to see and know about the poverty stricken individuals who lived in the roach infested area. The decision was made to move the last session of an influential convention from Memphis, Tennessee to Tunica to show support for the people living in Sugar Ditch. This shift created a need to bring in portable toilets for the convention, plus the residents there. The exposure did not stop at that. The TV show *60 Minutes* came and did a special on Tunica's Sugar Ditch. The entire nation was able to see the inhumane conditions that the residents were living in. What was heartbreaking about the situation was that thousands of federal grants had been allotted for the construction of sewer lines in the black areas, but it was used to improve sewer lines in the white neighborhoods. Large amounts of federal grants were also used to improve what is called "The Square." All the while a short distance away there were people who were pushed to the side as if they had never existed.

Now, only the memory of Sugar Ditch remains. The shacks no longer exist. Exposure to the deplorable conditions seemed to help improve the conditions for the residents there. People were able to get welfare which was of some help, but it did not greatly improve the conditions of the people nor did it help to remove Tunica from being the poorest county in the state of Mississippi. Many of the young people who grew up in Sugar Ditch did not allow their condition to interfere with their dreams. Many are college graduates, some are teachers, medical assistants, social workers, authors, business owners, or working in various areas of the medical fields. The blacks of Tunica County have not forgotten from whence they have come. Some have moved away, but they still pay tribute to this county in many ways. A club was formed called the Former and Concerned Citizens of Tunica, Mississippi (FC-COT). Every year, for the last 36 years, the FC-COT has held conventions in various states. The funds raised during these conventions are used to provide scholarships for young people to attend college. Over the years, FC-COT has been successful in helping young people to strive for their dreams, never give up, and to know that there are people in and from Tunica County who are working on their behalf.

The image of Tunica County has improved greatly. Over the years with the arrival of the casinos, the town of Tunica, Mississippi has been revived. Because of the number of casinos located there some people have named it, "Little Las Vegas." It is the third largest gambling center in the U. S. after Atlantic City and Las Vegas. Too bad our family couldn't recover like this!

It took some time for our family to recover from everything that happened. One thing that has stuck with me throughout my adult years is the thought that what if our uncle could have afforded the equipment needed to do the work on the farm? Since he somehow had given himself the position of being the head, what would he have done to us? Would we have been treated like the residents of Sugar Ditch? He already had the biggest portion of the money. With his hidden agenda, I shudder to think what he would have done if he could have gotten away with taking even more of the bigger portion of the profit. I know we would have suffered many more hardships than we had already suffered. He never would have tried to put any of us off of the land because we were the human laborers needed to get the work done. That was our assurance that we would stay put.

Chapter 24

A TIME OF THANKS AND COMPLETION

Upon the beginning of writing my book and even more so upon the completion of it, I set aside *"a time to remember"* the things that happened to us. Amazingly I have no regrets and I believe neither do any of the other children, about the things that happened to us as we were growing up on the land that belonged to our family. This has led me to a completion in my history that allows me to see that everything happened for a reason and we are all blessed because of it.

I want to say to the great, great, grand children of today, "You are blessed!" You do not know anything about laboring in the cotton field. You do not know anything about someone mistreating you and making you work for almost nothing, or trying to make you feel that you were worth no more than a piece of dirt. Your great grandparents, grandparents, and parents paved the way and paid the price before you were born for you to enjoy the life you are now living. You do not have to suffer from being whipped because it was believed that you were being lazy and did not want to work. All you have to do now is use your time wisely to get an education. You must get an education so that when you are grown you can begin to pave the way for the future generations of children who are yet to come. The opportunities are there. Reach out and seize these opportunities that are available to you. No one is standing in your way.

All of the things done to hinder us when we were growing up were meant for evil, but God turned it to be for our good. You may wonder why I would say something like this. It is because we had to work hard for everything that we got. I do not think any of us looked for handouts. We did not have parents who could leave us any money. They had only enough to keep their heads and their families' heads above water. They left us something more precious and more valuable than any material thing, and that was their LOVE. It is invaluable and no price can be attached to it. We, the grand children of God fearing and Christian grandparents are blessed beyond measure. We can all look back over our lives and know that we are blessed because we all have succeeded in becoming self-sufficient and contributing individuals with the help of God. We have all been able to stand on our own two feet by the grace of God and have carved out a successful life for ourselves and our families because we did not succumb to meanness and mistreatment. So, I will say from all of us, "Thank you Uncle Myers for how you treated us because you blessed us and you did not know what you had done. SO FROM ALL OF US WITH ETERNAL GRATEFULNESS, TO GOD BE THE GLORY FOR THE GREAT THINGS HE HAS DONE ------ IN OUR LIVES." AMEN!!

Acknowledgments

This book is a labor of love because the largest portion of the information was shared with me by my mother. Several family members, Ruth C. and Carolyn C., were able to add some information that was instrumental to the content of this book.

I am so grateful to my friend, Cherry L., for proofreading my book and making corrections where needed.

I would also like to thank Helen W., Rochelle S., Dorothy W., and. Jean W., for helping me gather important information for the completion of this book.

I thank my wonderful husband, **J. Edward**, for his untiring patience, love, and for taking on added responsibilities which afforded me time to work on my book without interference. I love him with my whole heart because he is a very good father, grandfather, and an excellent husband. He is a Christian, a family man, and the kindest man that I have ever known.

I am so grateful for my friend Esther J., who prayed for me and encouraged me to finish my book.

I thank my friends Lois W., Dorles J., and other friends who offered me words of encouragement.

I am grateful to my friends Thomasine L., Laverne C., Diane P., and Barbara R., for just being there if I needed them.

I thank my two grandchildren, **J. Edward** and **K. Janiece** who tried to be as quiet as possible while I was working on my book.

I thank Ed **W.** for all the times he spent working on my computer while I was working on my book and something would go wrong. He would so graciously come and repair whatever was wrong with the computer.

Last, but never least, I thank my God for giving me the strength to keep working on this book over the years when I really did not feel like going on because it brought back many sad memories. But I kept writing with the help of God. As I looked back over my life, the lives of my cousins, and my brother, I have seen from whence God has brought us. I gained added and renewed strength. I am so grateful to God. "I WILL BLESS THE LORD AT ALL TIMES; HIS PRAISES SHALL CONTINUALLY BE IN MY MOUTH." (Psalms 34:1, KJV)

About the Author

La Vellea Samot was born **in 1942** in Mississippi to the union of **J. H.** and **E. L.** Other children born to this union were **Willie J.** and **Felton W.** La Vellea graduated from high school and-received her Associate degree in Mississippi. She received her Bachelor of Science degree in Business Education.

After graduating from college, La Vellea moved to the Midwest. She still resides there with her husband of 46 years, **J. Edward**. They have one daughter, **L. Rochelle** and two grandchildren, **J. Edward** and **K. Janeice**, and one **great-granddaughter, K. LaRae.**

Several years later, La Vellea continued with her education. Before declaring a specialized area of study for advanced degrees she took graduate courses. She finally decided to go back to graduate school where she received her Master's degree and her Educational Specialist degree in Education Administration. These three areas of studies blessed La Vellea with the opportunity to have 90 hours above her undergraduate degree and moved her over into the Doctoral pay scale lane. After teaching for many years La Vellea was again blessed to retire from teaching in June of 2000.

Printed in the United States
By Bookmasters